WINDOW TO THE SOUL

Iris B. Struller

Just remember; each path is perfect in its own right.

Best wishes —

Iris

GOT THE MEMO PRESS

Window to the Soul

www.irisbstruller.com
www.gotthememopress.com

This book should not be used as a substitute for the advice of professional medical or spiritual counselors. You should never delay seeking professional help, disregard medical advice or commence or discontinue any medical or spiritual guidance because of information in this book.

Cover design by Iris B. Struller
Interior Layout by Iris B. Struller
Author painting by Iris Beate

ISBN 13: 978-0-9996682-0-7
LCCN: 2017918072

Got The Memo Press

Satellite Beach, FL

To JS, who opened the door

To MA, who picked up the baton

To AA, who will heal all

INTRODUCTION

I remember the day my mother handed me an audio cassette tape to listen to. She said it was one of the sessions she'd mentioned earlier, this one about my husband and me. I was intrigued and excited to find out what this entity, speaking through my mother, had to say.

For a period of time, my mother received insights, which she called her sessions, from an entity she sensed clearly. These visits occurred inside her mind and presented her with ideas about universal questions and ways of life. She explained that the experience was seeing pictures that she formed into words. She taped what she saw using a microphone and audio cassettes. As a story unfolded by way of these mostly early-morning sessions, she began to drop hints of their existence to me. After weeks of silence, she'd slide another fragment my way, mentioning casually the information she'd gleamed, summing it up in a handful of words.

Over time, she passed me some of the tapes on subjects she thought I would find interesting. An underlying trepidation was always noticeable to me. Would I believe her? Would I think she'd lost her mind? She warmed up to the idea of sharing this with others very slowly. Her major concern was being "found out," an impossible situation for her. As a medical doctor in a small town in Florida, she was afraid her patients would consider her a quack, a "crazy German lady doctor" and leave her for good.

That is what she impressed upon me when she handed me the case containing the remainder of her tapes. I promised to just transcribe them first. And I did so, slowly. Her heavily-accented English was familiar to me, her limited expressions haltingly moving along to form sessions that easily spanned twenty or thirty-five minutes or more at a time. Much of her language was clearly German-sourced, her own cadence of literary expressions dotted throughout, and I was sure no one would understand much of it the way it was meant to be. So I set about to edit them carefully, fully mindful to retain all of her original meaning. As I worked this rich earth, much like a plough slicing through its goodness, I would sense an inner green light when I got it right. Similar to a traffic light, the vivid green would fill my mind and I knew I could proceed to the next paragraph.

Once all the tapes were transcribed, I sat with her to find out more of what happened during the time the tapes came in, eliciting some stories of her daily life, the interaction with some of her patients. She filled me in, sharing bits and pieces, and, listening to her, I took notes, and read her expressions as she recounted her life. It was unusual for her to do this; she was an intensely private person. Still, she saw the importance and I came to more deeply understand how her experiences had impacted her. Her strong desire to remain anonymous, however, inhibited me in telling her story fully, openly, completely. Her great need for anonymity also opened my eyes to the privacy needs of others mentioned in the story: I have changed all the names, any situations involving patients or doctors are fiction and fictionalized. A session with a psychiatrist that I describe as her initial encounter with him is actually a composite of multiple sessions, leaving out the mundane and skipping ahead to the significant insights.

When we started on this journey, although I understood my mother's wish to remain anonymous, I didn't fully comprehend or appreciate what my changes meant to her. I was enthusiastic and focused only on her wish not to be recognized. When I created a fictionalized protagonist I thought to be very unlike my mother, and a character that turned out quite unlikeable, she hated the pages I faxed her, and said so. "This is how you see me?" Hurt and disdain seeped from her eyes into her voice, drowning me in guilt. "No, Ma, I'm trying to make her very unlike you. Didn't we talk about this?" I asked her to bear with me as I continued her story to the end. She still hated it.

Returning to the beginning, I reworked her character, softening the edges, sculpting a new personality. "This is too much like me. You must change it," she exclaimed when I faxed her the next draft months later. What to do?

I decided to take out her personal story altogether and just leave the sessions intact in the next version. The resulting skeleton was just that: lifeless, and hollow, a scaffold with nothing to hold. This wouldn't work. I put the manuscript in a drawer, knowing I had to rebuild her story around this core, for context, to make it readable, to make it mean something, to allow understanding to flow to the reader.

Mom passed away in 1998. Part of me felt the relief of her restrictions falling away with her passing, another was still bound by them. I picked up the manuscript again and again, working it here and there, but was never quite able to finish: it just didn't feel right. I put it back in the drawer before starting again in early 2000.

My father passed in 2004, unleashing an avalanche of personal challenges for me, marked by divorce, an intervention, emotional turbulence triggered by revisited childhood home and situations, guilt over my shortcomings in supporting my own children during this upheaval, followed by a new life direction, and overcoming my own health issues. *Window* stayed in the drawer, while another story took the forefront: the emotional journey triggered by my actions surrounding and following my father's passing.

I returned to *Window* in 2016, reworking it from scratch, using my earlier version as a guide and leaving the originally-edited sessions untouched, including any titles she had chosen for the tapes. Re-creating my mother's story and reactions, I've filled in the blanks from memory referring back to what she told me, what my parents both shared with me, how I've known them to be with each other and others, how they'd lived their lives and regarded those whose lives they touched. I've tried to keep true to their generous spirit, their way of life, the love they shared, and hope to have succeeded in that.

I have changed the names of anyone who is part of this story to respect the need for privacy of those mentioned in the book. The stories I wove of my mother's patients are fictional and only serve to transition into the session in question. Any similarity to actual events or actual persons, living or deceased, is purely coincidental.

In re-telling my mother's journey, and passing it on to you, the reader, I hope you will find inspiration in it. While it is part of my immediate story, considering how we are all connected, it is also a part of yours.

Iris Struller

October 3, 2017

CHAPTER 1

Waking Up

1989

There it is again, this hush of quiet that makes her hair stand on end. And yet, for the moment, her breathing slows, her heartbeat softens at its edges. And, sitting in her spot on the couch with the twilight blinking through the window shades, she relents, leans back, and allows this feeling to caress her.

“Hello, Harvey,” Erika says softly to herself, a quick mutter into her chest and she glances around to make sure Ruppert isn’t near. She’s not ready to divulge this, this sense of someone in the room, someone near whom she can’t see, even though she senses her husband might understand. At least she hopes he would.

She leans back and closes her eyes, wills herself to be open to the sensation that has become familiar: an odd sense of peace, a tranquility entering her chest and seeping outward into every limb. She breathes deep, slows her intake, breathes out again. In a moment it’s over and the shimmer surrounding her disappears. She sits a moment longer, still immersed in the otherworldly peace that seems to energize her being, so innocuous, and wonders why it is so out of reach at other times. “Thanks, Harvey,” she smiles into the ethers and picks up the magazine she meant to read.

And then, she turns into herself and takes another look. This sensation, it started with her operations, those ghastly nightmares that upsided her life. And she can’t get back to the ‘before.’ How did her life become so strange? Is this even real? In a blink, she sees herself running up the path, and her skin prickles with the movement of a thousand ants. What does it mean? Again, she goes through this film in her mind; the fear that comes with it now softened a little.

Breathe, she tells herself, just breathe. Still, her mind’s eye tells a story as a flood of heat blasts her face and she tries to cough the lump out of her throat, but nothing moves. Clamping her eyes shut to recapture calm into her limbs, she sees the fire lapping at her feet that race up the hill, acrid smoke searing the skin on her arms. She knows it’s just ahead, senses the heavy presence of this sacred temple even though the smoke is too thick to make it out now. Up, up, she must hurry, and she sees the flames are already there. *No! It can’t be!* A brusque shove from behind and she’s knocked to the ground, agony pinning her breath in her chest just so and she can’t move an inch. A bloodied blade sticks out her front, a vise of pain, and blood so much blood! Muscled arms are unable to move her body crumpled in place, all strength seeping into the packed dirt that cradles her head. She must breathe! With all her might, she pushes to expand her lungs, seared in this grip that rasps a gurgle amidst coppery gag in her throat, thick and sticky. Silent struggle fades her sight of the temple so near, and at last, her throat is clear.

She breathes in deep, unable to move in her chair, the images straddling her chest. *Quetzacoatl*, this strange sounding name is on her lips just like it was when she awoke from anesthesia, and she shakes her head in the dim light. What does it mean, this strange vision from her operation three years ago? What does it have to do with her, this odd scene from some place in Mexico? A warrior killed, the strange knowledge that she was him. And it keeps coming back to her, and even after all this time, she wants to know more, needs to know.

Yes, Ruppert's been a dear, this loving, kind man by her side. He scoured the Mexican travel books and even went to the library for her. That day sent chills down her spine, told her the image of the temples held her answer. But still, nothing. And still, more.

Her mind slides back to comfort as her body still resounds this gentle touch of no one "real." *Harvey*. A chuckle bursts from her lips. Harvey. She came up with the name because it reminded her of the imaginary rabbit, Jimmy Stewart's best friend from the 1950's comedy of the same name. She found it funny then, her own invisible friend. Harvey. He's been visiting her since the last of her operations.

She scratches her cheek, leans back once more into that dream-like state of floating, watching her own operation as if on screen. A surge of energy had pulled her upward. She remembers the weightlessness, the calm, the comfort, better than an embrace of an old friend.

She sees them again in her mind's eye, the four figures, light-colored beings, the soft glow emanating from each, was oddly moved at that same soft glow within herself. As they came closer, their lights melded with her own, and she wasn't afraid. She knew she could trust them, sensed love and spirituality, knowledge and wisdom. Old friends. Funny, she thinks now, how in that moment, all those details were so clear.

Hello, dearest friend, we meet again. Even now, she is smiling, filled with this incredible joy.

It's been so difficult lately. Is it over? Am I back?

Not yet, not if you're not ready: You've come a long way, you've accomplished great things, helped many people. In the latter years, however, you've returned to a well-known path of materialism, which is easy to do in such a materialistic learning place as Earth. But this time, you wanted to accomplish so much more, so much more spiritually. You set such high goals for yourself. You haven't quite accomplished those goals yet, so you have the chance to go back and try again. If you want to. If you feel up to it.

The big house, the luxuries, the material possessions she had accumulated: she knew what they meant instantly. She always thought all those long hours of helping others balanced that out.

You have time; you can become more spiritual. Through your spirituality, you'll have the chance to open the door for others, thereby completing your own lessons. You can reach the goals you set for yourself, for your own experience, your own growth, the type of development we talked about before you entered this lifetime. You can reach the next level, where you want to be. It's up to you.

Will I have the strength? I've felt so alone lately.

It won't be easy. It will be hard but you can do it, you have the strength to do so. You won't fail, you won't be alone. We'll be by your side at all times, as we have always been. You'll feel our presence more strongly than you have in the past, we promise you that.

Even now, she wants to believe it. She wants to do it. She wants to succeed.

If you want to go back, you can go back. Finish what you started. Same body, same life. Make it different. It's up to you.

And then, she was whisked away by epinephrine entering her body, and the bleeping of the hospital machines was the next thing she remembered.

She takes a breath, gets up from her chair. She knows, somehow, this is not the end, this is some new beginning. And somehow, she senses, this part of her life won't be so much about herself, no matter how packaged. For a moment, a thread of fury slides through her. Hasn't she given enough? What more can she do? As a doctor helping others, whether they can pay or not, she helps them. If she can't beat the cancer, how can she continue her work? How can it not also be about her? For a split second, she wonders if even this thought is selfish.

And she's reminded of the promise, the promise she clings to now. *You'll feel us more strongly than you have in the past, we'll be around you, you won't be alone.* And she takes heart, clings to that, allows herself to believe. And she walks to the kitchen to start dinner.

CHAPTER 2

Opening Doors To Acceptance

1989

Erika approaches her husband as he pours the last of the coffee into a cup, and rests a soothing hand in the middle of his back to announce her presence. “Ruppert, I’ve made an appointment with the therapist. The one Michelle referred me to." The words spill quickly towards the last threshold and she mutes her voice. "He's a psychiatrist." Funny, saying it has left an odd tenderness within her, and she's not sure why the words would have this impact.

"A psychiatrist?" A fleeting concern has pushed his eyebrows a fraction above their normal resting place, giving his eyes a comical bracket, somewhere between disbelief and wonder.

"Yes, I've been thinking about this for some time, struggling with it, really," she says now, staring at the coffee machine as she fits the filter in place and begins scooping the grinds. She turns to him. "You've been wonderful with this," she says, pauses then, a curious torment edging into her. "I need to, I *want* to speak to someone outside of us; so many conflicting thoughts inside my head, I need some input, a different perspective altogether. I think we're both out of our league; I know I am. I no longer know what I'm feeling, I've struggled with dark thoughts, don't know where they come from. I've never had those before, not like this. And those images, the ones from Mexico, won't leave me." The waterfall has rushed over the edge, taking with it a tender part of her, and she's again startled by this inner anguish. She steps back quickly, retreating to safe distance. "Some input from outside might shed some light." She squints as she turns to face him, bringing his blue eyes into focus, the joyful crease on each side of them behind glasses, and she pushes aside unease over rejecting him in this role.

"You don't think we can work this through ourselves?" He has slowed for a moment, observes her more closely.

"We've tried so long to find explanations ourselves, but it doesn't seem to be enough. It's not getting me the answers I need. I'm sorry, I don't mean to minimize all our efforts. You know how much I appreciate your support, and I love you so much for it, but I think this is bigger than us."

"Ok, I get it, I understand," he says then, holds onto her eyes with steady gaze. "You know you can always talk to me," he adds. It's a casual tone that's submerged any sense of betrayal, she senses, and pushes her further along.

"I need to do this," she says with much softer voice. "You know, this guy apparently uses hypnosis or regression or some way of getting into the past. I'm not sure I'm sold on that, but maybe there's a way he can crack me open?" She chuckles a nervous hiccup, avoids his gaze. "I want to try, want to be open. I need to find out; this is making me nutty! I know you're here for me, but I think I need a fresh pair of eyes on this, a different insight. I'm sorry, I'm rambling? My life seems upside down; I need new perspective." She turns toward him directly. "Reassurance, maybe? I guess I need to know I'm not losing it." Her face distorts into a split second crumple before she recovers.

And he embraces her with tenderness in his response. "Ok." He nods her into his chest. "You know I support whatever decision you make."

She smiles softly at him. For catching her, for holding her, for being there. "I know. I love you for that." Relief flicks at her lips, chasing tense eyes, and finally softens the edges of a tightness in her bones.

* * *

A few days later, she enters a comfortably furnished office that walks the line between professional and inviting meeting place and sits down opposite the slim man in his forties.[1] Intelligent eyes assess her from behind round spectacles, and she finds herself breathing a little easier. She likes this man already.

"Three years ago, I was diagnosed with breast cancer. I went through moderate mastectomy and reconstruction. The anesthesia never agreed with me and I had severe reactions."

---

[1] What I describe here as one session is actually a composite of multiple sessions.

She slows, reaches for the glass of water, takes a sip, and recollects herself when she replaces the glass on the table. "I decided to handle this on an outpatient basis. I didn't want anyone to find out. I was worried my patients would leave and I'd lose my office. I'd only just opened my practice in town. And anyway, who wants a doctor with cancer?" Even now, she stumbles and hisses the word, this death sentence. She shakes her head, a rustle in the air. "I couldn't take the chance. My mother died of colon cancer discovered too late." She slows again, searching for words. "I don't know what to do anymore." Stillness settles in the room after her words, and she's looking at him expectantly, partially deflated and exhausted by the effort it took just to describe this part alone.

At last, he moves. "Erika, you know I use hypnotic techniques in my therapy to help my patients through very difficult experiences. I've had very good results. You seem so very distraught at the moment, and I'm wondering if some of the relaxation techniques wouldn't be helpful to ease some of the tension you're experiencing now." He leans back guardedly, watches her.

"Is that possible? I mean, really possible?"

"I could guide you through it, perhaps it might help you."

She takes a moment to touch this idea, and finds herself wanting to embrace this possibility that sounds almost a little too easy in a way. But, what if it could help? She inhales deeply.

"Ok, I'd like to try it."

"Alright, why don't you sit back in your chair, take a deep breath and listen to my voice. You may close your eyes if you wish. If not, focus on something in this room, say the figurine of the two little birds here on the bookcase. Can you see those?" Erika follows his eyes, nods then. "Just look at those, let your eyes close a bit so the birds go out of focus just a bit and just keep looking at them and relax, just let the tension go."

"Now, focus on your head, let the tension go out of your head." He pauses, giving her time to do just that. "Now, let the tension go out of your neck, feel it flow out. Now your shoulders, let the tension flow down your arms and out of your hands and relax your arms." He pauses again. "Now feel the tension drain out of your chest, your abdomen, and your legs. Just let it drain out, let it all go out."

Erika can feel the tension trickle from her, mellowing her energy throughout her body as she follows his words. She seems to empty out, the stillness of a pond seeping in to replace the chatter. As she waits for further instruction, she lets herself float within.

Instantly, a faint hiccup trips her throat shut and she can't breathe. She tries to cough, but it won't dislodge as she wrestles with it, a breath for air the only struggle, but her throat is fitfully closed.

"Erika, Erika! Erika, wake up."

Booming voice filters through the darkness, pulls at her and she startles, opening her eyes. She clears her throat easily then, finds him leaning forward in his chair. "What happened just now?"

"I think the tension may be overwhelming for you at this time," he says, his voice returned to reassuring monotone. "I think we should wait a while before we try this again."

She leans back, takes in a deep breath, and lets it out completely. "My throat closed up. What does that mean?" Her mind has tripped over the moment of no air, and she can feel it even now, and it frightens her.

"I think your situation is so great for you that you may have panicked the moment you relaxed enough to give you the sense of losing control. An anxiety attack, perhaps," he says, his voice smooth and distant, yet perched and present. "Because you were doing really well and seemed to be able to completely relax and able to let go, until that crucial moment. But that's ok. It shows us that you are able to let go of the tension. In fact you relaxed so completely you were almost in a light trance." His clear eyes are focusing on her, and she thinks she notices mild surprise at this accomplishment. Then he jots down some notes, a few erratic movements onto the pad on his lap. "How are you feeling now?"

She sits still another moment, scanning for words. She knows she needs to answer, but she's still unsure. "Ok, fine, I guess. I don't understand how my throat could close so completely. Why would that happen? But, alright, maybe an anxiety attack could explain this? I've never had one of those before. Could it be something else?" Her eyes are on him; he is putting his pad on the table next to him.

"Let's talk more next week."

"Oh." She can't hide her disappointment, tempers it quickly. "Oh, ok." She stands up, gathers her things. "I'll see you next week."

* * *

It won't leave her alone, but she doesn't tell Ruppert, not yet. It doesn't seem right to burden her husband with this, this strangeness that pops up everywhere and surrounds her. He's been through enough with her. *What's going on with me?* She pushes nagging doubts under before they have a chance to form inside her head, keeps focus on her workload, muffles inside screams until they quiet. Until the next appointment finally comes.

"I trace some of this back to my second operation," she says while looking at her therapist squarely as he picks up his pad to write. "When I came out of it, I had some sort of flashback or something. Everyone tried to convince me it was a dream, but I don't think so." She leans back, tendrils of thought streaming into consciousness, devoid of color, and then, bursting.

"Who was trying to convince you?"

"Well, my doctors for one, and," she hesitates a moment, "Ruppert, too." A nervous chuckle tickles her throat, a faint shudder cloaking her memory. "I don't think he knew what to do with all of that. I can't blame him." She retreats, then presses on. "Even I have my doubts on some level, but I can't let it go. It's so real, so familiar, like a memory. I can barely grasp it, but it's there, present all the time. I can't seem to shake it. I find myself questioning it relentlessly." She glances at fidgeting hands in her lap, stills them by clasping them together. "And since that operation, other strange things have started happening." She shifts her body uneasily. "I sense . . ." She quivers softly, almost unnoticeably. "It feels like someone is around me all the time." She shrugs, shakes her head again, this subtle tremble to shake off this doubt. "I don't know if I'm just imagining things, but I sense this energy or presence or something. It's very real to me, like the feeling you get when someone has come into the room and then you turn around and see that person. Only I never get to see it." She rubs her eyebrow, hiccups a soft grunt, clamps her lips. "I've felt it now every day since that operation, for five to fifteen minutes at a time. It's like I'm visited by Caspar the friendly ghost. Or Harvey." A faint chuckle, and there's a true joy creasing her cheeks.

"Go on," he says at last, this neutral presence observing in the stillness.

She takes heart to tell him all, decides to fly over her fear of sounding odd, dives in. "It started with the experience I had coming out of anesthesia when I was a warrior of some sort, trying to reach this temple, and I think it had to do with Mexico, because I saw that temple in a book on Mexico Ruppert dug up when we got home."

His eyes rest on her, the quiet in the room stretches uncomfortably.

"Is there a way to find out more?"

He studies his notes, puts down his pen, looks up at her. "Let me ask you this," he says, settles in his chair. "What are your thoughts on reincarnation?"

She blinks, holds his eyes. "I believe it's possible," she says at last, self-assured. "I've been reading books that have shown me more of this possibility. Ruth Montgomery and the Seth books."

"Does this idea frighten you?"

"Living again? No, not really."

"Ok, well, the reason I'm asking is that there is a way to find out more. With hypnosis and regression, we could try to place you at the time prior to the incident you've remembered to see if there's anything else."

"We could?" Hopeful, and then, something in her pulls back urgently. "Let me think about it. It's a big step. I don't know if I'm ready."

"That's ok. Give it some thought. We don't have to do it today." He shifts in his chair, relaxes somehow.

She watches him, stuck in this ramble inside her head. Suddenly an urgency grips her tightly, nudges her again. "No, let's. Let's do this today. Is that possible? I have to find out what happened to me, what's happening to me now. I need to know. Please help me find out." She seems to hold her breath again, that pause in time when her expectations rise and she's just waiting.

"Ok," he says casually. "You're ready?"

"I am." She shifts and settles again in her chair, finds a comfortable position, listens to his words guiding her to relax each part of her body, just like before.

And, instantly, her throat closes. Holding off the stench of fear and burning flesh, she grasps herself into sitting still within the now familiar scenes of flames and pain and death. A surge of energy, and she's pulled up and beyond.

His voice comes through and she opens her eyes. Her mind replays pictures; she tries to hold onto the details. Stillness within her, then the calm of understanding floods the empty space.

"Ah, I think I know now," she speaks almost automatically, her mind lagging on all she is sensing. She pushes away from it a little, works to focus on him. "Thank you. I understand now," she says softly more to herself than him.

"Can you talk about it?"

She replays snippets in her mind to guide her. "What I understand is that I was the last of my tribe, the rest had been killed. Spaniards had discovered our village and plundered everything. They'd found out about the gold we'd hidden for Quetzacoatl and wanted that too. They'd already tortured and killed so many. They'd burnt the village. I'd gotten away but they came after me. I was running to the temple. I'd kept the secret and I knew that if I reached the temple, Quetzacoatl would save me and reward me with everlasting life. I couldn't believe it when he let them kill us all. But they never got the gold. That secret died with me."

He's taken notes; she pulls into herself.

"What are your thoughts?" he asks.

"It was so real, so very real." She looks at him with eyes gazing as if at stars. "I understand what happened now. This wasn't a dream. It feels like I really lived through this." She seeps into herself, following images still lingering, this silent film of some other life. Then, a snag. "Could I have made this up?"

After a moment's consideration, he shakes his head deliberately. "I don't believe so. At least not from what I saw as you were in trance. I know you felt everything you saw. I do believe this was an experience from another life, and I suppose the anesthesia woke it up in you."

"Really?" She tilts her head, narrows her eyes. "A memory then?"

"I believe so, yes." He leans back into his shoulders. "This is not so unusual, Erika. Anesthesia has been known to affect people in all sorts of ways. You've heard about out-of-body experiences? Well, they happen during anesthesia as well, many times without the person knowing about it."

And as the words straddle her mind, she feels floaty, as though she stepped into peanut butter, and the walls are moving fluidly toward her. She gets up, needing to escape quickly, needing to breathe.

CHAPTER 3

Stepping Through The Door

She's not sure how she's gotten home as she unlocks the door and steps into the cool twilight of the house. She fills a glass with ice and water and gulps it quickly; the cool embracing her head in gentle breath. She fills the glass again and takes it with her to the couch, leans into the cushions and puts her feet up on the other side. Almost immediately, the sense of comfort surrounds her, a nesting into embrace beyond the softness of the pillows. Fleeting images of Mexico pass her eyes, and she rebounds, resounds with this new understanding.

Then, she flings open her eyes. *Who's there?* She scans the room, an urge to write pushes itself into the forefront, this need for pen and paper, and she searches the room for both. *Is that how you want to communicate?* Her thought is instant, an unspoken request within her. She gets up, collects some sheets from the kitchen counter, picks up the pen she sees near and returns to her place on the couch.

She gathers herself, stays open, hovers her pen ever so lightly across the top of the page, breathes evenly and deeply. *Go ahead*, she invites and listens into the stillness.

She waits, and still, nothing. "I need your help," she says then through closed eyes, allowing her pen to keep hovering over the page. And as she relaxes her body in waiting, she notices impulses, fragments of feelings coming to focus, and writes down what she senses.

". . . helping, giving strength, peace, relaxation, floating. . ."

She pauses, looks at the words. Her hand feels a little stiff; is she so anxious to get it right?

She inhales again, opening just a little, tenderness embracing her, floating her thoughts, and she allows this feeling, relaxes into it without question, and images come, swiftly, smoothly, vivid. The urge returns and prompts her pen into action, lending words to impressions she receives, and it glides across the paper without any effort at all.

"We are explorers from another galaxy, from the direction of the Milky Way. We are lost; our exploration has gone awry. Our group consists of ten to fifteen ships. We lost power and had to float to this planet for an emergency landing, hoping to survive.

"The gravity of this planet, the third planet of the solar system, is pulling us down. We are having trouble breathing and moving. We are sending signals to our friends to warn them not to come too close, knowing that otherwise they will be caught, too. We will return to free you, but you must stay away. There are two of us. We look around; the planet looks inhabitable for now.

"We have to stay here until we can repair our ship. We have difficulties breathing and walking and the sun's rays are hurting us. We must find tunnels to hide in. We can move mountains and stones with our thoughts alone.

"We sense that there are animals and primitive inhabitants who are small and naked and have spears. We are tall, of light color, almost lucent.

"We are trapped. We cannot take off. Our mind power cannot overcome the gravity of this planet. We know that another ship has crashed. We have to find them and will have to wait for the return of the rest of our group. We have to build signs so they can find us.

"Venus, green emerald, why did you lose your eternal way?

"We communicate telepathically; we know each other's thoughts and feelings instantly because that is the creation of our lifeform and our reality. Our ships are energy circulations formed for transportation by our thoughts. They take us wherever we want to be in the universe and return us to our home galaxy.

"Star Sirius was our temporary operating station. We live without time, we use expanding thought realities as our experience and for our learning process."

The flow of images and thoughts pauses, and she waits into it. As her eyes stray over the paper, she resists breaking her relaxed focus to read it, marvels at what has come out of her, knowing, at the same time, it isn't hers. Curious, she remains still, holding her pen ready over a new sheet. And as the energy shifts, the comforting feeling blends out, is replaced by the simple empty space of her living room. She puts down the pen, and leans into the cushions, eyes holding the table in front of her.

At last, a stir within her. *What is this? Can this make sense?*

She looks at the pages she's just written, this scramble of words poured out of her unhaltingly just a moment ago, a waterfall, relentless, and, still, it doesn't seem to be hers.

What's going on? And in that moment, thoughts collide, slices of memory sweep into her sense of the unmistakable.

"Harvey? Do you have something to do with this?" She listens into the silence; her heart throbs loud within her chest. "Come on, answer me!" She twists in her seat, a frown etched in her brow, arms clamped across her chest. And then, it comes, this unholy calm that overtakes her and presses gently against her, this hug she feels undeniably and through its weirdness it brings her peace.

She exhales, a final push after a marathon of holding her breath. "Oh god! Oh god!" she wheezes, sobs dispersing the tension tearing out. "Oh god!" She stares at the pages. "Thank God it's you! You scared the hell out of me. What is going on? What are you doing?" She sits a moment longer, and, at last, touches the pages, her eyes glued to the words, and she reads them once more, as if for the first time. She puts them down in front of her, pushes them away, shakes her head in disbelief.

"What on earth do you want with me?"

CHAPTER 4

More Questions Than Answers

She hears the kitchen door open, some shuffling on the counter, and knows Ruppert has come home.

"How did it go today?" he calls out.

She turns so she can see him, hooks into his eyes. "The strangest thing happened just now."

He comes closer and she sweeps her arm above the pages in front of her. "This," she points, holds his puzzled look, answers the unasked question.

"I don't know what it means, either." Open palms motion back and forth from the pages to herself, stuttering in mid-air. "I decided to ask Richard Colin to regress me after all, and he did, today." In her mind, she quickly retraces her steps to the earliest point that still makes sense. "I don't know if this is related to that." She searches his eyes, feels her own clouding over as she follows ribbons flowing through hands, losing contact. "It started out well: it seems he was able to hypnotize me. And, well, I'm not sure how it happened, but I started back at the place, that burning place, with the same pictures I saw when I woke from anesthesia."

He sits down at the foot of the couch, eyes on her but far away. "What? I'm sorry, I'm not understanding, tell me again? You let him regress you. And what happened?"

She slows her breathing, folds her thoughts into submission, stifles an impatience within. "You didn't hear me? You weren't listening," she says softly.

"No, I heard you fine: I'm not *understanding*. Tell me again."

"Ok. He regressed me," she starts again, then slows, searching for words. "It seems I returned to the same place, the same images I saw when I woke up from anesthesia after my second operation, the one where I saw myself as the warrior in the fire." She has enunciated each word evenly, ignoring the welling up of tears in her eyes, hates this weakness within herself, and spaces her thoughts with utmost care, observes him again. "It seems, the anesthesia may have set off something, opened a door to a memory from another lifetime or something like that, that's how he explained it. It's odd, confusing, just so strange." Her glance slides over the papers on the table and back to him. "I'm not sure exactly," she searches his eyes, retreats, "how valid this is." Again, she hesitates. "There's more," she says, grimaces as she pushes the pages toward him. "I wrote this about an hour ago. I came home and felt lost and so I asked for help, from whom, I don't know," she lifts her hands, circles them. "From the universe. And then I felt this need to write, an inner urging." She collects the pages, stabs them at him. "This is what came out."

He takes them from her, and she watches them leave her hands with a soft shake of her head.

"It's not mine." She has jabbed out this defense, softens instantly. "What I mean is, I don't think it's *mine*, specifically, if that makes any sense at all. I mean, I don't think it came from me. I can't explain it. I don't know what to say. I don't think this came from me, but it came *through* me."

Ruppert sits perfectly still as he starts to read. She watches him; he's pinched his eyes together, keeps reading. For a moment, he looks up, a cross between question and doubt and something else she can't make out stitches across his face. And then, while she waits, she sees him in a different light, remembers the first time she laid eyes on him back in 1955, in Würzburg, Germany, where they both went to medical school and she was desperate to join his study group. An unexpected smile flicks the corners of her mouth upward. The others were doubtful, but he pushed it through, believing in her. Then, that rainy day when examinations were scheduled, and she rode the back of the old motor scooter sideways, lifting her feet high to avoid puddle splashes from soaking her new suit, while balancing the umbrella over them both as she held onto him. They passed the exam; the orals had been tough. Can he believe in her now?

A frown knits her brow as unease shuffles into her. "I'm not sure what to think." She chuckles nervously while his eyes continue their trek across the page. "Is it my imagination? Those Ruth Montgomery books I read, did they influence me?" He glances at her for just a moment, returns to the paper, continues to read. "I felt a comfort, an energy just before this urge to write, Harvey was back," she jitters on. "It was comfort, I'm sure of that, and somehow it prompted me to relax, ease up, try to let go of this tension I've been carrying around, and, part of me was sure, I had this feeling that everything is going to be ok."

He puts down the papers, turns to her, sits there, silently. At last, he stirs to speak. "I don't know what to say." He slows, shifts in his seat. "You've been through a lot. Who knows what the anesthesia induced or unleashed?" He nudges his shoulders. "I don't understand this, I have to be honest. I don't know what this is. If you're helped by it, well, I don't see how it could be harmful. My thought is, take this to Richard and see what he says. Maybe he has an opinion on it. Me," he pinches his lips into crooked uncertainty, "I'm not sure what to think. I don't know what this is, really, but I'm here for you." A pause for breath, and she finds herself easing away from the blade of anxiety that has sprung into her core, stuck deep in her chest. "I'll support you any way you need, you know that. We'll get through this together, whatever it brings." She hangs on his voice, this soothing salve meant to smooth a wrinkle.

Still, she is tattered. She manages, "Thank you, thank you for helping me, being there. I'm just trying to understand what's happening with me." She sweeps a hand across her forehead, claiming the hair matted to it before her eyes reach the water outside the window. "The feelings I get are a reassurance, love, understanding," she offers. "It's the oddest thing, and yet it feels like the most natural thing in the world, as though I know it, have always known this feeling. And, as I was writing, it was pictures I saw, a slide show almost, and it's those I wrote down as quickly as possible. I don't know what's going on, I don't understand why it's happening. I get the sense it has something to do with patience and faith for now, and maybe understanding later on." She faces him directly. "I want to be open for this, but, really, I don't understand it at all."

"Ok, well, see what happens." He shrugs a note of discomfort, and she senses his loss for an answer. "Maybe this is just a one-time thing, maybe you got it out of your system. Maybe Richard can shed some light on this." An uncertain smile, her cheeks tug in response.

A twinkle returns to her eyes, a glimmer of mischief. "I've called it Harvey, Harvey's my friendly ghost."

He snorts. "What? Oh, ok, so now we have a houseguest. Harvey. Funny." He turns away.

"No, not funny," she says, pins him in place with the hush in her voice. "*Real* to me." She squints at him, urgently. "No really, I need to tell you, I need you to know. I think it's some kind of, I don't know, *perception.* Some kind of *sensing.* I *sense* a presence, that's all, some sort of energy that's *real* to me, that's a comfort to me in a strange way." She looks at him directly. "I know it sounds odd, but it's something that's been helping me through this, in a way. It's like a knowing that all will be ok, a confirmation, a support, if you will. Oh, it's just so hard to explain." She nudges her head into her shoulders, turns away.

"Like some kind of divine intervention? Ok," he succumbs. "I get it, Erika, I do. I'm not making fun, please believe me. It's just, there's been so many strange things happening, forgive me, I'm trying to accept all that's been happening, too. I'm trying to understand. This is new for me, too. It's so different from before."

She smiles weakly. "I know. This is hard." She lets out a soft chuckle. "Maybe we have some help from the ethers, or the universe or wherever, if you will." She turns into herself. "It's *real* to me. It's been visiting since that operation with Mexico." She shrugs. "I've been afraid to tell you."

"Afraid? Oh no, don't be. Please. You know you can tell me anything."

"Yes, I know. I realize that and I know that, but I couldn't, can't, couldn't. It's been hard coming to terms with this, and, really, I don't know where I stand even now. I'm sorry. I know I'm not myself. It's been terribly overwhelming. And I just couldn't explain this."

"Well, you're not alone. You're not alone in this. We'll do this together. In it together. I'm here for you. I promise," he says, pulls her close and wraps his arms around her.

"I love you."

"I love you too."

CHAPTER 5

Stepping Into Unknown

An unusual spring chill has crept into the house and Erika pulls the blanket more tightly around her shoulders. Sounds from the kitchen: Ruppert juices oranges. Then, quiet.

She leans back, decides against the magazine on the table, looks at the pool, shudders at the chill. Then, warmth, the familiar greeting she instinctively leans into, smiles. "Harvey's back."

She scans for Ruppert, notices the slight hiccup in his movements. "No need for alarm," she says. "It's just comfort, it's reassuring to me, really." He's put a glass of juice in front of her, pauses again as though debating a thought, returns to the kitchen.

How can she help him understand? This feeling, it feels like home, like she's not alone, that all will be alright? She shrugs it off, finds herself easing into the soft of the comfort embracing her shoulders.

Then, again, this need to write. She reaches for the paper left on the table from the other day, hunts for the pen under the magazine.

"I miss you. Feeling of strength. I love you too.

"I want to show you the world, the universe, the cosmos, and the oneness of us all as part of the cosmos.

"I want to show you our home. I want to show you galaxies and dimensions that have no time, space or forms, where our thoughts build and change everything to our pleasure and needs. I want to show you our way, our infinite being. I want to show you places filled with love, where hatred, lies or other negative human behavior doesn't exist. Places, where our inner strength allows us to be ourselves, where the thought form, the expression of the soul, the spark, exists as intended by the master of the universe.

"Although we have come from far away in space and time, we share the same past and the same future. Together we *are* the future. Open your inner self for messages, thoughts and events, even if you lack understanding momentarily. In time, you will learn to contact us, your teachers. We are from and for your future, which is and was our past, present and future as well. We will present our knowledge to you in moments like this or in dreams, as your window to our world. Learn from us.

"You, as humans, know the reason for your existence but your ego's material thinking suppresses this knowing. Don't forget that your earthly life lasts only a second in our time. You exist according to the laws of the ever-expanding universe, which is filled with the vibrations of love from the consciousness of all souls, of all living beings, of all times. It spans millions of years of your time and includes past, present and future.

"Try to think in terms of love. Unselfish love will automatically bring peace to your inner self, which will reach your ego and your outer self. In turn, you will radiate eternal love and peace into your surroundings.

"To ensure the continued evolution of the human race, it is essential for mankind to learn love in its fundamental sense and to overcome hatred, negativity, violence, force, and horror, which will lead to war. At your present development, war would mean nuclear war and destruction of yourself and your world. For us, the warning came too late; we could not stop the destruction of Atlantis ten thousand years ago. We are learning from our past mistakes in another dimension and warn our brothers and sisters to live in peace with each other, in thought and deed.

"Thinking is energy and energy does not get lost. Just as you cannot keep your thoughts back, you cannot recapture them once they leave your mind. Thoughts travel indefinitely as energy in other dimensions, where they live as living reality and wait to be transformed to matter. More highly developed beings than yourselves have the power to materialize those thoughts and use them as substances to create their own reality, much like stones and plants are materialized ideas from the thoughts of previous generations.

"Thus, as living and powerful reality, and although unseen by your eyes, the compound thought of the human race forms and changes the world. As humans, you are the population with the highest level of consciousness. As such, you are responsible for the consciousnesses of any less developed species or population. This is cosmic law. If you radiate power, force, horror or terror in your thoughts, you create counterparts of matter which radiate back and fulfill those thoughts in material terms. So, please be careful with what you think, because you can easily fill an entire dimension with your thoughts."

"Who are you?"

"Joseph, Gioseppe, Alfonso, a name does not matter. I am, as is your inner self, attached to the universe, your teacher, your contact, your friend. We are a group, each with our own life experiences, present and future. You cannot sense us unless we make ourselves known. We are timeless, as you will be when you have fulfilled your cycle.

"Don't be afraid. Make peace in and with yourself and accept your ability to receive information and messages from us. We are joyful to have found you to express our thoughts and will contact you again. Joseph.

"Contact is joy and happiness."

She senses the shift in her perception; the room seems to empty out. Erika hovers her pen over the paper a moment longer, but is sure it's the end of the message. She relaxes her hand, a stillness enveloping her mind and being.

Ruppert comes into the room and she contemplates him as he sits down in the chair opposite her. He catches her watching him, slides his eyes across the pages.

"I just got this," she says, and points to them. "I only remember the gist, but it has to do with the universe and our connectedness to all, and, well, I'm," she slows, her mind a spin, "I'm not sure what I feel. Astonishment, really."

He reaches for the pages. "You wrote this just now?"

"Yes," she says, shakes her head quickly. "Similar to last time. It came through me. It was a flowing of images, in a way," she shrugs quickly, "that I put into words and wrote down." She drifts off, her gaze on the pages. "A lot like last time, really, but this time Harvey gave me his name. Well, a few of them; he says names don't matter."

She notices an unreadable flicker of surprise across Ruppert's face. "Ok, I'll read them. Is that what you want me to do?"

"Please." She turns to the window, gathers the many little pieces that seem to be herself, pulls them together again. "I know this is such an odd thing, so unlike anything we've ever faced." She slows, hovers over her thought, "until my operations." She turns toward him. "I need you with me in this, please believe me I've not lost my mind. I've stepped into, it feels like I've stepped through another world, I don't know how to explain it. I'm filled with wonder and don't have the words to describe it."

He has gone quiet as he pulls the pages onto his lap, shuffles them into order and begins to read. Then, a sound, barely a breath; he slides down the words, slips a glance at her.

She inhales deeply, a sigh softens her posture, deflates tight girders around her. She reaches across the table. "Here, please take the pen, and date this. March 22, 1989. What's the time?"

He checks his watch. "Just 7:30," he says and jots it down, and she leans back into the cushions, watches him read.

"What are your thoughts?" He asks her when he's turned the last page.

"I'm not sure what to think. It seems pretty amazing to me, and I don't understand it at all, but I feel connected somehow, and it seems important to me." She shrugs. "I don't know. I'm sure I'm not making this up. But I feel good about this."

He nudges his head, a soft tremble sideways, then a gurgle. "No, I agree with you, I don't see how you could be making this up; I didn't know you had this in you. This is," a smile chuckles from his lips, "quite something." He slides the pages back across the table. "If this can be, if it's true, it's fantastic. But, I have to tell you, I can hardly read your writing. It's almost illegible."

"What do you mean?" She stretches for the pages, fans them as she looks. "Well, I did rush."

"Yes, but some of the words are really hard to make out. I wonder, if we should type this before we lose it. Hey, what if *you* were to type instead?"

"Type this? Or you mean the message when it comes in?"

"That was my thought. Why not? If one comes through. That way nothing would be illegible. Make sure nothing gets lost."

Her face falls, then sets tightly. "That wouldn't work. No, I don't think that would work. I don't think I could do that."

"Why not?"

"Oh Ruppert, do you really see me at the typewriter?"

A moment's recognition subdues his eyes and he scans the room, explores other possibilities. They come to rest in the far corner. "What about a tape recorder? Speak into it?" He doesn't wait for her answer, gets up quickly and disappears down the hallway.

"I've found it! And batteries. Now we just need a cassette. I'll be back." He picks up the keys to the car, jingles the door. She watches it close, listens to the sound of the turning lock, shakes her head, sits back on the couch.

CHAPTER 6

Joseph And Ophelia

March 23, 1989

Erika is aroused from deep sleep in a cloud of comfort and love. Through drowsy mist, she reaches for the recorder Ruppert has set up on the nightstand, finds the microphone and slides fingers to the 'record' key.

"Joseph, you've returned! So has the memory. And the old feelings," she says, voice somber, eliciting images through the dusk in her room.

She starts slowly, haltingly, but images and ideas persist. She forms the words to describe what she senses. "They were all on drugs to overcome the fear and induce a feeling of well-being to make the leaving of our home, Atlantis, easier. This pretense enabled us to load our ships with everything we needed for our journey and new starting point: our knowledge, instruments, food, water and medication. All packing was done in great secret to avoid panic in the unsuspecting people around us.

"We knew our country would soon break up and we were the last knowledgeable priests who could lead the people out and who could, if necessary, reach other worlds, similar to our planet. It was our mission to transfer the people of the continent as colonists onto new parts of the planet, or onto new planets, in peace and love, so the scientific and biological heritage of our world would not be lost.

"While we were joyful over our ability to leave as the last ark containing the knowledge of our home, we hoped to be united again in the spirit of the new worlds, as part of the new worlds. We were headed toward a foreign land, a new starting point, on ships that were powered by crystal energy and could carry us through water and air."

"Good-bye Joseph, I know I have to leave you, my love. I am Ophelia, the daughter of the king. Our destinies separate us, but our minds and thoughts will keep us together, as will our final destiny. We will communicate telepathically as we always did. And once we have reached our goal and started a new colony, we will reach each other again, somehow."

"Goodbye, my love. My ship is waiting – so many have to be transferred – I have to leave. We will name our destination Egypt, and will build pyramids to house our knowledge. When the time is right, these storage homes, the temples of our knowledge, will be found again. You will stay in Mesopotamia and find a race with whom the last of us can multiply, like I will.

"We have the strength because we are the old ones. We are those who came from the stars so long ago, traveling through the cosmos and settling here after flying with the wind of the sun, the wind of the stars. We will travel again to be part of the evolution of the galaxy."

"Goodbye, Joseph."

"Ophelia, my love. I wish I could stay with you. I will miss you so much. But we'll live with the knowledge and our acknowledgment of the future, the past and the present. In a future life, we will once again live together as we have until now.

"If we cannot stay on this planet, we'll leave and colonize another. Which one? We'll find out when it is time. You will know when to leave, which group you will lead and who will go with you, Ophelia. You are strong enough.

"Remember, we have the knowledge of our previous lives and of our future life. We can tap into it and receive the understanding we need."

"I'm afraid, Joseph."

"I know, I am too, because we don't know what will happen to us. We may survive as our minds alone, with the knowledge of our future life . . ."

* * *

She rewinds the tape again, replays the end. It clicks to a stop at the same place. She opens the recorder to examine the tape, finds it has run out of room at just this stop. She leans back against the pillows, must come to terms with this simple fact: the message ends there. Erika sits still, notices an ancient ache within her returned, its muted edges so real, so present. Had they not checked the tape properly? How could this happen? A blur of an image in her mind, thousands of people crowding a harbor in the dark of night, and she remembers the moaning and yelling and singing and chanting all at once, misted in confusion. She takes a deep breath and wills herself to move, limbs weary and heavy, but she must get up to get ready for work.

Ruppert is in the kitchen, pouring coffee. "Would you like a cup?" he asks as he offers her the one he's filled.

"Thanks," she murmurs and takes a sip. "A message came through. I listened to it again, but the end of it is cut off – the tape ran out, I don't understand how we could not have rewound it properly. Was it an old tape? Anyway, I ran out of tape, and I don't remember what he said." She's moving rapidly, puts down her mug. "It spoke of a very frightening time."

He takes milk from the refrigerator, adds some to his cup and returns the carton.

Sensing ambivalence, she says, "I don't think I'm making this up." She's shaken her head quickly, steps back, reclaims her coffee from the counter and takes another sip, "It's quite a story. I know we need to leave for the office, but, would you listen to it?"

"Now?" he has slowed. "Do we have time?"

"It's really not very long."

"What's it about?"

She thinks for a moment, tugs out her chin. "Atlantis. Well, more of a mass exodus from Atlantis just before its destruction." She shrugs. "I know it's unexpected, considering, but it leaves me thinking, stunned, really. I don't know. I wonder."

"What?" He's softened, turns to her before glancing at the clock.

"I don't know, it's all so unreal to me, and yet it's right *there*," her hands cup the space in front of her, "and I'm the one creating these tapes of these stories, these, I don't know what to call them. I just don't know."

He slows, puts his mug on the counter, checks the clock. "Ok, I'll listen to it." She goes quickly to retrieve the recorder, presses 'play' before she hands it to him. As her own voice fills the room, she balances at a threshold toward that snippet of reality floating alongside her own singsong.

"Hmh." A muffled doubt, stifled in the clacking of the tape coming to a stop. "That's something," he musters, and she can't read his voice as he puts the recorder on the counter and picks up his mug.

Another breath of silence, and she beckons herself to speak. "Do you think this could have really happened?"

He shakes his head, "I really don't know. I can't explain it, have no answer as to what it could be." He looks up at her. "Maybe Richard? At your next session? Do you have one planned? It seems other-worldly to me, and I don't know what to make of it." He slouches a sheepish grin. "I'm sorry, I just don't know." He slows, then perks toward her. "What happens to you when this comes through?"

"I see images. Same as with the writing. I'm prompted to put them in words, if I can say it that way. It's all very quick, like a slide projector on full speed. I'm not consciously thinking while I'm speaking, it's as though I'm following a thread and I know what to say. It's almost automatic, I don't search for the words, they come on their own." She slows, reconsiders. "I know this is strange, but I need you to believe in me." She picks a crumb off the counter top. "I guess I somehow opened the door when I asked for help last time, but this time I didn't. I was woken up from deep sleep, and I knew a message was about to come through, and I knew I needed to be alert for it, that it would be important. But I didn't know what would come through." She finds herself shifting in her seat, searches his eyes again. "Kind of like reading a newspaper and you don't know what the headlines are." A sigh escapes, she feels pushed into the deep side of the pool, and it occurs to her that she never knew what she had wished for, yet here it was.

"You know, to be honest, I want to find out more," she says then, determined. "This history of Joseph and Ophelia, this story of Atlantis, there's hope and such pain. Such love."

"Should I worry?"

"What, about this? About Joseph? Don't be silly." A flick of the wrist mimics quick jerk of her head, and she's waved him away.

"What is it, though? Do you have an idea?"

"No, not really." She turns again to face him, clear eyes clouding over. "All I know is that this has been happening since the anesthesia; I'm changed somehow. Maybe it opened some kind of door, some other perception. I don't know." She scans his expression, shifts her gaze to the floor without latching onto anything in particular. "I don't think it's anything bad. At least I don't sense it to be."

When he walks away, she watches him for a moment longer. Then she picks up her keys, turns, calls into the empty space left behind, "Ruppert, do we have any books on Atlantis?"

CHAPTER 7

Atlantis

April 3, 1989

Erika is summoned from deep sleep.

"Good morning, Olivia. 6 am Monday.

"I'm glad you convinced Erika to continue with us. I heard her and your earnest wish to work with us in our plan and destiny.

"Erika wanted to know about Atlantis. You know it already, Olivia.

"Atlantis was an incredibly beautiful continent that flourished from twenty-thousand to ten thousand years ago in your time frame. It stretched from the Spanish East Coast, the site of our large harbor filled with ships for travel across sea and sky for trade with other parts of the world, to what is now the Atlantic Ocean, to the coast of Florida, to the Bermudas, a now destroyed part of the continent, and to the Canary Islands, which contained hills and mountains.

"We were a highly intelligent race, tall with fair complexion. We had highly developed souls and had reached a stage of rapid soul and spiritual development, while others had turned to materialism, building beautiful palaces filled with precious art objects and monuments. Ornate decorations of pure gold and silver lined the walls of their houses, which were painted in wonderful colors and contained murals of scenes with delicate figures. Monuments lined walkways as testimony to our magnificent organization of human beings.

"We traded gold and silver coins, as well as our knowledge, with other, primitive countries, that had all the earthly things we needed and wanted for our lavish lifestyle: gold, silver, copper, and other metals, as well as coal, cotton and silk. Peace reigned in this society of balanced material and soul growth.

"It was our goal to live as promised to Adam and Eve in Eden. We wanted to be like Adam and Eve, in the image of our Creator. We knew they had been banished to Earth, as a learning place, because they wanted to be His equals. To make up for their mistake, we wanted to devote our lives to Him. We sought to worship our Creator, who fulfilled our every material wish as well as our quest for cosmic knowledge and beauty.

"Our Creator gave us knowledge by enabling us to reach other more highly developed humanoid consciousnesses on other stars and galaxies with our minds alone. Groups of our scientists trained their highly developed mind power so that, together, they could transmit themselves to other galaxies with their minds alone, and became our ambassadors to those worlds. Balancing give and take, they were able to exchange knowledge covering every part of awareness. Thus, we became both a teaching and learning population.

"The minds we contacted taught us science and brought us the sounds of the stars for incredible and unbelievable sounds of music. They taught us solely for the sake of our own continued development. They gave our artists ideas for unbelievable art, which they expressed in paintings to reflect our state of development and bring us glimpses of eternity. Since it was our goal to live in more than one dimension in Atlantis, we gladly received the stratospheric cosmic sound and art.

"With this art, they showed our population the inhabitants, animals, plants and humanoid developments on other planets and in other dimensions. Our poets filled our libraries with poems of sagas of the future in devotion of our almighty Lord, to whom we wanted to return in gratitude, bringing with us our culture, science, and accumulated knowledge as a gift. We wanted to offer Him our music, our poems, our statues, our art, pictures, sketches, and treasures as thanks for letting us live in a paradise just like Eden.

"Our state of development enabled us to build ships with mind power alone. We were able to rotate and transmit matter as energy form to break through the atmosphere and travel through space faster than light, using nothing but our highly developed mind power.

"In fact, as thoughtforms, we traveled timelessly through space and time. We wanted to reach other similar, highly developed human lifeforms in other galaxies with whom we, as thoughtforms, could communicate. Using telepathy to exchange thoughts and knowledge, we were happy to transmit ourselves, together with them, into the next dimensions. This brought us closer in awareness to the almighty Creator of the universe.

"However, in our midst, a group, equal to us in their state of development, decided to misuse their power by changing the thoughtforms of their mind power not to honor the Almighty but to exert force. They used their power in form of leadership of the nearby population. Eventually, they enslaved them and enjoyed their superiority and power over a people who adored them as gods.

"By purposely keeping the consciousnesses of a less-developed race at lower levels to make them a cheap and willing workforce for themselves, they broke the law of teaching and trust. According to that law and cosmic law, the higher developed consciousness is responsible for the less developed consciousness and has the obligation to teach and thereby enable any lower consciousness to raise its level of awareness to the teacher's level in the voluntary process of learning.

"This failure was the beginning of the never-ending cycle toward negativity and contrary to the law of creation. We had started down the same path as Adam and Eve.

"The seduction was too great for the many who became ever more attracted to this misuse of power, which, in the end, corrupted our race. In their need to destroy, they abused atoms, molecules and cell structures of advanced life forms. Against the will of that lifeform, they isolated consciousnesses of its structures, and broke it down into its components of molecules and atoms. They then manipulated and transformed its consciousness into a deadly and destructive weapon to be used against others.

"This manipulated composite grew into an enormous negative lifeform of destruction, which eventually got out of hand. In the false belief that they were creators of incredible power in the image of the Creator of the universe, they were proud of their accomplishment and thought they were invincible.

"Ultimately, their actions lead to explosions of crystal and atomic powers, which were the outbursts of the negatively manipulated consciousnesses. The manipulation had created negative expressions that were not compatible with that lifeform's consciousness and caused its eventual destruction. This was followed by the destruction of our world, a world that had itself destroyed in conquering other worlds. Its leaders thought they were creative gods, but were in fact false images of the Creator of Life.

"We were not them; but we were defeated. We knew the destiny of Atlantis was out of our hands. We tried to reach outer space by sending ships across water to reach other continents, which we knew to be undeveloped or little inhabited. Parts of us knew we could survive there. We planned to start over in primitive surroundings, with primitive but normal compounds of atoms and molecules. We would elevate the primitive consciousnesses by teaching them about our lifeform's mind power. Thus, spanning hundreds of years, we started to teach our culture and history with the goal to build a new Atlantis, or rather, a form of it.

"Others were not so courageous. Using the last threshold of combined mind power, they transmitted themselves to other planets in their desperation to build colonies for survival. Many lost sight of their goals while trying to preserve our ways, knowledge, learning and experience. Some reached another dimension in which they were able to live as consciousnesses. Those were the most highly developed priests, who, trusting their compound conscious ability, transmitted their souls into other dimensions before the destruction started.

"We are a group of those who reached their goal and helplessly watched the destruction of Atlantis. Although we could not maintain any contact after the explosion destroyed all life there, we could at least observe some members of our group form what is now Egypt, where, in the last desperate use of their ability, they built the pyramids. These monuments, as expressions of a highly-developed race, were an effort to reach consciousnesses in space and other dimensions by using the radiation these structures produced.

"They were trying to reach consciousnesses on other planets with which they had previous contact, calling on them for support, help and to teach, so as not to lose everything they had known. Some groups made it to the Easter Islands, as reflected by the monuments. Some reached areas now known as China. Take a look at certain meridians on planet Earth. In Indochina, Mexico and South America, you will find cultural developments that started out of nowhere and are still unexplained by your present culture. The Egyptian pyramids and stone henges are testimony of the final memories of a wasted, highly developed race. In Crete and Greece, the ideas lived longer and created other ideas and ideology of a previous presence of gods.

"However, the gateways to other dimensions shut down during the disturbance caused by the horribly invasive explosions of the stratosphere around Earth, which shot images of warnings to other worlds to stay away to avoid damage to themselves until the radiation had settled down, which required an immensely long time in the earthly time frame.

"Thus, we lost our contact with other planets. Eventually, we also lost the knowledge to reach the stars during this time of pure survival. The memories of the knowledge were not passed on to the children of the remaining few of the original race. Retaining partial but not full memory, they were able to continue the development of their consciousnesses from the point of destruction forward. However, this meant that they had to start their development from the level of a living cell, and grow from the consciousness of compound living cells to a learning consciousness with the urge to free itself of material matter and to reach the picture image for which it was created. Many got discouraged, only few, very few had the inner strength and knowledge to form the intuition to follow the path, steadily energizing the recreation of the image of the Creator which was meant for any lifeform that starts its development from the consciousness of an atom-molecular structure.

"As we followed the development, we tried to guide their growth by bringing to life ideas in highly developed persons, which were the revived memories of our former state of mind and development. They were our gifts of love, vibration and memories to propel the positive development in an attempt to balance the negativity that had grown so strong on Earth. Just think of Michelangelo, Rembrandt, and of the ideas of flying machines at a time that was, as you may think, too early for their state of development.

"Consider the leaders of the Inca, of Egypt and Atlantis. Consider the ancient rituals of tearing out the hearts of animals to sacrifice to the gods, which was primitive knowledge of cardiac implants, which previous "gods" knew and did. Think of pharaohs who were buried in pyramids in a certain North-East position and prepared for eternal life, a consciously remembered Atlantean knowledge of the eternal lifeform.

"We sent messages to planet Earth through Lao Tse, Confucius, Buddha, and Christ, as mirror pictures of Adam. You can call them reincarnations of Adam in their knowledge of being part of the Creator. They knowingly held the wisdom to radiate the image of the right path into their environment. By living in that image and radiating it to one another and into their surroundings, they were able to avert another Atlantis-like destruction from learning place Earth.

"Nonetheless, destructive atom consciousnesses remained, which eventually compounded to molecule consciousnesses, and, in turn, compounded to negative and consciously destructive lifeforms who infiltrated human thoughts and grew to primitive thoughts of being god-like. You can see this recorded throughout history, in leaders of cultures and religions, who were not spiritual leaders but materialistic ones. In their greed for power and money, they followed the path to destruction instead of leading creative forces and lifeforms. Inevitably, they could not balance the creative and destructive ways in the direction of the creative forces on learning place Earth.

"Since then, the scales have never balanced out; they mostly point to the negative, heavy-debt burden side. The further the scales fall toward the moral debt burden, the quicker destruction will follow, finalized by the complete destruction of planet Earth.

"Are you satisfied, Olivia? You know it anyway from your previous you and as knowledge received in Interspace. For you, Erika, it is new in a certain way. Look at it as a learning experience, along with other teaching material you will receive from us. Try out some questions next time. Ask me anything which might strengthen your consciousness to follow your path to our combined goal.

"Thank you, Erika. You're reminding me more and more of Olivia. Olivia becomes stronger and stronger in you, a blessing for your soul and consciousness.

"Love you both and see you tomorrow morning. In love and remembrance, Joseph."

CHAPTER 8

Treading Carefully

A momentary pause has snagged Erika's mind and she shuts the microphone, carefully placing it next to the recorder on the nightstand. Images continue to crowd her as she moves through the din and out to the living room where she hears Ruppert juicing oranges. He looks up at her and she comes closer, reaches for a mug in the cabinet above.

"Another message came through," she says, wrapped in tenderness, crinkles her brow and reaches for coffee. "It's about Atlantis. I've been waiting for something all week. Finally, some more details, some more evidence of its existence." She turns to look at him and smiles triumphantly. "I knew it!"

He's turned slowly, faces her, a pause hovering between them, when at last he forms the words, "Atlantis? Erika?" He looks at her intently, hesitates. "Honey, I'm really not sure what to think about this. You seem so convinced about its truth, about this 'reality' you believe you've uncovered . . ." he pauses again. "Love, I'm not sure what to think, but I am somewhat concerned."

"Why?" She looks at him askew. "What do you mean? What's there to be concerned about?"

"You really have no idea, do you?" he says and pulls her closer. "This is all very strange to me. I have to be honest. Half the time, I'm not sure what to think. Everything's turned upside down just a little. I mean, Harvey? All these messages? I'm not sure what to think, how to process this."

She steps back, searches his face, her own covered in unreadable mask. "I thought you were ok with this? I thought you were with me on it?"

"Of course, I am," he says quickly. "I'm just not sure what it is, what it means, how to process this."

"Too otherworldly for you?" She pokes his side, tries to smile, beckons for more.

"Well," he hovers in space, slows again and she can see him thinking. "Yes," he says at last. "It's not that I don't believe: I believe in you, I believe this helps you get through all the uncertainty, but I just don't know what to think." He steps back a little, his arms dropping by his side.

"Well, would you bear with me? Listen to the tape? For me? I know this is new and it's a lot, and it's strange and unsettling and all those things, but would you listen for me?" She holds his eyes steadily with her gaze, and the world seems to have stopped spinning.

He contemplates her for what seems to be minutes. "Of course. Of course I will," he reassures with kind focus in his voice, and she's picked it up and she wonders if he is just petting a lost puppy to make it feel better.

She pinches her eyes, steps back from him, takes hold of her mug of coffee to take a sip, decides then to just push forward. "Well, this session, if that's what I can call it, is about Atlantis." She searches for words and finds herself holding her breath again through heavy chest. She inhales deeply to break this awful spell. "It seems it's a continuing story, a part of another lifetime." For an instant, she smiles into herself before his uncertainty folds back into her, and she holds her mug tightly while she faces him head-on. "It's such a beautiful love story." She shrugs, stands still to read his expression and give him a chance to respond. "It's ok, really. I'm not losing my mind." When he doesn't speak, she moves to walk past him and towards the bathroom, cup in hand.

He hesitates; she can feel him just standing there. "Am I reading too much into this?" He asks and she turns around. "My concern is that, well, maybe you're getting too close to all this. I know you want to know about Atlantis and its possibility, especially since that TV program reinforced the mystery of it all, but, maybe, you've been thinking about it a lot, and . . ." he pauses, torment hovering in his entire demeanor. "Could that have influenced you and that's why you have this 'session'?" He looks at her, beckoning her to talk, and she finds his words have hit her hard. She sees the shift in him, is still unable to move. "I'd like to hear it, of course, I'm happy you're willing to share it. But, please keep in mind that your eagerness to know more may be influencing these messages." She holds herself in place; she must listen, she must let him talk. "Look, I'm trying to keep an open mind, especially since this is so important to you. No, I don't think you're crazy, not at all." His eyes caress through knitted brows from behind glasses, a subtle comfort she soaks in quickly. "I'm still grappling with this, trying to come to terms. I want to be open. I don't know what this means, Erika, I just don't know. But I believe in you. I love you and I believe in you." Part of her shreds in relief, a sudden shiver passing through her. "And yes," he says, "I will listen to the tape."

"Thank you. I appreciate that." She says, starting down the hallway before turning back. "Thank you for believing in me, for trusting me."

* * *

They arrive at the office just past eight. Ruppert heads to the lab, Erika steps into her office. Her nurse follows close behind. "Morning, Doc," she says quickly. "You already have someone waiting for you."

"Already? Something wrong?"

"I don't know. He gave me his name as Roger Wolf, says you know him. He wouldn't tell me what it's about, said it's a follow-up. He doesn't have an appointment, and I checked the computer, but he's not in our files."

"He says I know him? Wolf? Doesn't ring a bell." Erika takes a look into the waiting room, smiles at the man with silver-speckled hair kept busy by a young girl, instantly familiar. "Give me two minutes, then send him in."

Shortly after, the door opens. "How ya doing, Doc?" His broad accent brings a smile to her face. Jim McKeagan

Five years ago, food poisoning brought him to her on his road trip to Miami. Since then, a few times when he's passed through, he's stopped by to say hello.

"I'm fine, question is how are you? What's going on?"

He sits down on one of her burgundy chairs, shifts in his seat instantly, his hat tightly in his large hand. "Well, I'm here to get a second opinion," he says, fidgets again with the envelope in his hand and his hat's bill. Erika waits, observes him quietly as he seems to be searching for words. "I had an operation about six months back, and a car accident a few weeks ago. My back's bothering me badly the last couple of days."

"You had surgery?"

“Yes, I brought my X-rays,” he says then and slides the envelope across the desk.

Erika studies the film. “I’m afraid this is beyond my field of expertise. I’d like to refer you to a neurosurgeon, that is, if you’ll be here for a while.” He nods. “I’ll have Sylvia make arrangements. You’ll need your X-rays with you.”

“Sure, that’d be fine,” he says, pauses, his eyes straying before focusing on Erika. “I asked your nurse to keep an eye on my daughter in the waiting room,” he starts stiffly, shifts in his seat.

“That’s not a problem,” Erika says, waiting expectantly. “What’s wrong?”

His boisterous bulk seems to deflate in the chair opposite her as he reaches for his eyes, swiping at them, and they somehow seem hooded when he lets them go. “I don’t know what to do,” he says then. “I think my daughter’s been molested by my ex-wife’s boyfriend.”

“What? Are you sure? Do you have any proof?” Erika’s entire system has gone on high alert. “Did your daughter tell you?”

“No, nothing like that. But she’s acting funny, something is off. Something isn’t right. I don’t want to accuse anyone if I’m wrong, but I don’t think I’m wrong. I have no evidence, nothing yet, I haven’t even spoken with her yet. I’m not sure how to start, how to go about this.” He falls back into himself, and Erika can see how he’s holding himself together. He looks up at her and squints sheepishly. “And hey, I’m sorry about the name. I don’t want anyone to know I was here, not until I’ve had time to think this through.”

“What makes you think she’s been abused?”

“She’s acting differently since he’s moved in with her. She ran to me like she’s never done before, ever. There’s a fear in her that I can’t put my finger on. Something is very off, something is very wrong.”

"You've ruled out a conflicted sense of loyalty? This couldn't be guilt over another father figure having moved into her home?"

"I don't think so," he says quietly.

"You haven't talked with her yet?"

"No, I haven't. I'm not sure what to say. I don't know how to start the conversation."

"How old is she now?"

"Nine."

"Ok, well, ask her directly. Ask if she's been touched inappropriately, if she was told to keep a secret. If you have nothing else to go on yet, talk with her about her school too, or friends' houses, where she spends her time. Go slowly with the questions, but ask the questions. If you have any concerns, I can refer you to a social worker to speak with, or a child psychologist. Has her doctor examined her?"

"Not to my knowledge. Nothing like that yet. It's just a hunch I have; there's a fear in the girl, an anxiety I've never known her to have before."

"Alright. I'm going to give you the number of a child psychologist I trust, who's very good. I want you to call her and tell her what you've told me. Start with that today. And please, if I can help in any way, call me."

"Thank you. I needed to get her away from there and was hoping you could direct me."

"I wish I could do more." Erika finishes writing down contact information. "I've also written down the neurosurgeon's info."

As Jim sits back in the chair, Erika picks up the phone.

* * *

Early evening, Ruppert and Erika drive home together.

"Oh, what a horrible day," she exclaims at last. "And I'm in a terrible bind."

"What happened?"

"One of my patients came today to speak to me in confidence about his young daughter. Messy divorce that dragged out terribly, and today he told me that some time ago, his ex-wife moved in with a boyfriend."

"Yes?" He glances at her pained expression, she's shaking her head out the window, massages her temple.

She's tenuous about continuing, hesitates again. "He suspects the guy's molesting his daughter. Well, he doesn't know for sure, doesn't know at all, really, but thinks something's wrong." Again she pauses. "I've known him for a few years now, and I take his concern very seriously. It's not a custody tactic or anything like that," she says and her lips have disappeared in thin line. "I don't know if he's jumping to conclusions because he's angry, but I don't think so. This was despair I saw today. In any case, I've referred him, but I haven't reported this as of yet. I got a hold of Virginia and she's agreed to see them tomorrow. He came in under a false name; he needs some time to think, wrap his head around this idea and all."

"How well do you know him?"

"Well, only the times he's come into the office, but well enough." Her hands rub against her thighs, she settles further into the seat, exhales a loud whoosh. "I don't know what else to do."

"You've referred him to a psychiatrist."

"Yes."

"Alright then, you've done your end. Call him in a day or two to follow up."

She nods into the blue of the sky whizzing by outside the car. "Yes, that's what I'll do. Ok, yes. Thank you."

CHAPTER 9

Old Bonds And Promises Of Old

Late in the evening, Erika finds herself still holding the shards left by her patient's concern. Lying in bed, her mind fills with sorrow and anxiety and she can't let go of any of it. As she tries to settle, familiar perception slows her and she reaches for the microphone at last.

"Your disappointment in people's behavior reflects the disappointment you felt in an earlier life. That's why you were so hurt at the broken trust and promises you heard today in your office.

"You remember the broken promises you and soul Stephen experienced in another life, at a time when you were both too young to make your own decisions.

"In 1840, you were both very much in love and wanted to get married. But because of your young age and his parents' need to move away, you were unable to fulfill your wish.

"You had met on one of the first ships traveling to the East Coast. However, his father decided to move westward where land was more plentiful, in hope to find a better life.

"The loss originated the longing between your souls. You felt as though something died inside you when his parents, mainly his father, would not let you come along. Although you admired and loved his father, to some extent you hated him too. You knew he had decided against taking you because you were too small to be a useful worker and it broke your heart.

"In another earthly life you were a charming and emotional young woman with many suitors, each of whom offered his love and affections. However, you were unable to truly love in return. So, you flirted casually, not meaning to hurt anyone. You thought everything existed for your pleasure alone, including others' feelings, and you took them for granted, while your feelings for others remained superficial.

"In that life, you lived at a French Court. Your parents were upper class, which placed you at a high social standing. You spoke French, German and some Italian. You played the mandolin, the piano and spinet.

"I remember the poet who loved you, and whom you eventually learned to love through his poems, because they reflected real love. Through him, you finally learned to discover real feelings, contrary to the superficial admiration and life you had experienced until then in your environment of upper society.

"You died young and returned to Interspace. Reflecting on your life, you realized that it lacked spirituality and we decided that you would benefit from a spiritually fulfilled life. You were also so dismayed by your behavior in that life that, *this* time, you chose to live two incarnations in one life to make sure you would progress and not waste time again.

"To ensure you would follow through, you made a pact with the souls around you, who are now Ruppert, Iris and Stephen.

"Stephen was initially reluctant, having just returned from a very difficult and strenuous life full of disappointment and despair, in which he had to fight for survival beginning with his first few moments of existence.

"In that life, he was an unwanted child and had to work very hard, physically. Hoping to escape the despair, he joined the army at fourteen. However, he was not ready for the horrors ahead of him. At his age, he was physically unprepared for the cold and rough life. Emotionally, he was neither prepared to see others killed, nor to hear the moaning of those who died helplessly on the battlefield, themselves unprepared to die so quickly.

"He couldn't understand why his comrades would not help each other. He was overwhelmed by the unrelenting struggle for survival, and fighting for an idea he did not believe in. It was an idea to kill the wealthy, an idea he thought was stupid. As a refined soul he was used to doing the right thing, respecting a lifeform as it was. His beliefs did not include mistreatment or injury to others.

"Yet he found himself part of a group which fought and killed indiscriminately – children, women, men, anyone who was rich or who could not convert to their idea. It was an idea of revolution and equality, an idea they hadn't yet mastered themselves. They didn't *free* the souls, the people, they didn't give them equality. They killed them.

"They took from the rich to enrich themselves, they brought cruelty because they themselves were cruel, they marred and tortured others because they were tortured souls. Some tortured out of frustration over their inability to change the system, others because they enjoyed the power. They swept across the Eastern

Front of Europe, feeling the power and bringing terror, pain, torture and unnecessary death.

"In the end, he was killed by one of his own comrades because he could no longer accept the revolt against the system. In his final moments, he had to live through the same physical pain he had involuntarily inflicted on others while believing in an idea to free the world and the people. It was an idealism he initially had not been able to resist because of his youth, and when he finally did resist after discovering the pain it brought, he paid with his life.

"In Interspace, he saw that he needed a life for soul growth and decided to balance this life with one of love, understanding, awareness and giving. Both of you needed lives contrary to your previous ones. To help you reach your goal, you met soul Ruppert, who was at first reluctant to live with you again in earthly life, but finally agreed because you had lived happy previous lives together. You felt the forces of love very strongly between the three of you. You also discovered that you could recharge each other's souls and could teach each other what you had not learned previously on planet Earth. You, Erika, wanted a glimpse of their previous life.

"You chose your parents because you wanted to become a doctor to help others. You reasoned that having a father as a doctor would enable you to focus your ideas from the beginning to complete your own lifeform by helping other living beings in their need, solving pain and anxiety, and healing the physical body so that the spiritual part of the body, the soul, can develop.

"Through the experience of others, you learned of the torment in the soul. You learned about anxiety, fear and terror. You learned what power can do to human, animal or plant life, or to any lifeform on your planet when evil directs it. You witnessed destruction and the mistreatment of animals, plants and humans caused by the power of a handful of souls. You heard about the terror and horror of imprisonment. Although you were personally sheltered from it, others taught you this truth using various languages and expressions.

“You realized then that, as a physician, you could comfort others, physically as well as emotionally. Providing this support made you outstanding in a certain way. And with help from other outstanding ideas you unknowingly learned about soul Stephen’s suffering in a previous lifetime and soul Ruppert’s suffering in another part of the same country.

“That was the seed within you to become a physician. It developed you into the soul you are now and gave you the ability to grow toward your present state of understanding and awareness.

“See you in the morning, if you’re up to it. Love, Joseph.”

Erika shuts the recorder and leans against the pillows. At last, the string of the tenuous refrain has broken inside her head, replaced now with rich sounds of other cadence. She lets her eyes roam the room, settles on the window softly pounded by the rain. A flash illuminates the leggy palm that sways in rhythm to cymbals crashing crescendo before rolling into the distance. Dark shapes shudder, bend under the weight of shaggy crowns. She pushes aside the lace curtain hugging the window, looks through the pane sweating descending streams. Eerie peace between bangs, the ancient oak a silent sentry, the silver river spikes the darkness beyond: these pieces are like a frame to her existence. A distant light twinkles steadily across the water, a beacon winking at her, and creases her cheeks into a smile.

CHAPTER 10

The Search Continues

Erika startles awake through images flashing fire above the Elbe River in Dresden, phosphorus-fueled sprites dancing across the water, and exploding inside ancient walls, insatiable. Sitting up in the darkened room, she listens to the quiet, keeping still through muffled fog of sleep that holds glaring imprints within her mind. Ruppert had shared snippets of his experiences as a youth of 16 trapped in his country's warfare years ago; why was it back so real now? She prods her mind to alertness, pushing out her husband's story of racing through fire-rimmed streets.

Joseph, help me, her single thought and she leans back against the headboard breathing deep, and still her mind won't let go. At last, she turns on the light.

What was it that has occurred within her? Is she really part of something incredible? Is there a greater meaning to her life than all this?

She slows for a moment, lets her eyes wander the walls, silently waiting. Then, she takes in the time on her bedside clock. He won't visit today. At last she gets up.

Another regression. The thought sidles in, a tagged flutter stays behind, and she decides to schedule the appointment.

*　　*　　*

Elisa

Erika takes her seat in the office, familiar now with its bookcase housing the delicate ceramic birds that threshold other views, settles while Richard turns on the recorder.

"Ok, just take a deep breath or two and allow yourself to relax now," he says, his monotone guiding direction, and she holds onto it to glide into different domain. "Just get very comfortable. Take a moment or two and let your mind wander through your body and make sure everything is comfortable and relaxed. And when you feel ready, tell me verbally."

The silence stretches. "Ok," Erika says at last.

"Excellent. Now open your eyes for a moment. Find something to look at. Over on my bookcase is the pair of little owls. Can you see those?"

"Yes."

"Look at the eye of the smaller one, the reddish brown one. Try and focus your eyes on that eye. Set your eyes much like you set the lens of a camera, focus down tightly. Begin to see that eye to the exclusion of other things and you'll sense a hazy sort of appearance as you continue to stare and as the hazy sort of appearance begins to form and things begin to become sort of obscure, your eyes get very heavy, Erika. And as your eyes get heavier and heavier, there's a stonger and stronger desire to close them, so just let them close and drift. Drifting is going to be easier for your now . . ."

"There's a castle! There's a beautiful castle," says Erika.

"Tell me about the castle."

"It's white, whitish. It's fading. I lost it."

"Relax. Give yourself an opportunity to be open and perceptive. Drift deeper. Allow your mind to open to whatever memory is there, and wherever you might be. Allow yourself to drift now. Allow yourself to be open. Don't force or try anything."

Silence floats for a few moments. "I see a church, a gothic church with a beautiful entrance. Small. People are going in and out. There are nuns – they look like nuns. There's a carriage. There are horses."

"Where are you standing that you're seeing this?"

"I'm looking from above. As though I'm flying. Why am I flying?"

"Like flying?"

"Like flying. Flying over hills."

"Can you look at yourself? Do you see anything?"

"No. I see only the hills. I see a stream. And back there are the sisters, the nuns, and their little gothic church. They're bringing – what is it? A coffin. They're carrying somebody out. And they're putting him in that carriage. There are two brown horses in front of a carriage with a driver and they're taking it to the cemetery with the big oak tree. There is a priest, an open grave. People have gathered around it. And again, a lot of nuns. I see them weeping. The priest is talking. And I think I'm in the grave now. Yes."

"You think your body is in the grave?"

"Yes."

"Has the casket ever been open that you can see it?"

"Yes."

"Describe what's in the casket."

"An eighteen year old, about eighteen year old beautiful girl. She had wanted to become a nun. She has very pale skin and she looks so peaceful."

"Her hair color?"

"I cannot see her hair because of her habit. Black dress and a big cross on her chest and a white band around her forehead. Her hands are folded as though she is praying and the black dress goes down to her feet with black stockings and black shoes. And she's very small and she looks so peaceful."

"Do you know why you died?"

"Poison. Something poisoned."

"Something you ate at the convent?"

"Possibly, I don't know."

"Listen carefully to the language of the priest. Is it familiar to you? I know it would be familiar to you as the person alive."

"I don't hear anything."

"You know that they're talking but you don't hear anything."

"I don't hear anything. Was I deaf?"

"Can you go back … go back … see the carriage in front of the church, see the carriage empty in front of the church, as you began. Can you go back any further?"

"There's that castle again, but this time it's greyish."

"Can you enter the body of this beautiful girl? Can you go back?"

"There is that greyish castle again. Like a castle, perhaps it's a ruin now and a big tree and a lake nearby and I'm playing with friends there. I'm about twelve years old. We are climbing the tree very quickly and we are doing it just like the boys. And it's so much fun."

"What is your name?"

"Elisa."

"Elisa. What are you wearing, Elisa?"

"I'm wearing a long dress, down to my ankles. It's blue. And there's a little collar around my neck and I have long sleeves and I have brown hair and blue eyes."

"And the other children laughing and playing and climbing the tree?"

"Oh, we're playing together and there are some boys. And the boys are wearing boots and tight slacks with white shirts with collars. There's that castle again and I'm inside now."

"Is this tree you're climbing in the courtyard outside?"

"Yes, outside the castle. And inside is marble and chandeliers and ...oh, and I have to behave."

"You have to behave when you're in the castle?"

"Yes."

"But outside the castle you can play?"

"When I can sneak out, yes. When I sneak out, then I can play with all the children there. With the children of the servants, but then I have to go back."

"What is your father's name?"

"Adolbert."

"Is he a good father to you?"

"Yes."

"Is he strict?"

"Yes, and he is a big man and heavy."

"Can you see what he looks like, what does he wear?"

"He has a funny hat with three edges and he has a feisty face. He's around forty or forty-five, very heavy. Boots, tight slacks, and a white shirt and blue jacket."

"Mother, can you see what mother looks like?"

"We have a picture of mother, in an oval frame. She has dark hair, dark eyes an oval face and her hair is wavy and put up . . .

and she's very graceful and pale and very slim and her dress is beautiful. It's a long white dress, white sleeves, made of a very thin material – silk, like a veil so thin, it has to be silk – and she's beautiful. And she loved me."

"She loved you? Or she loves you?"

"She loves me. She plays with me."

"But you only have a picture of mother."

"She's not here anymore."

"Are there others around?"

"Servants, and a bigger older lady. She's wearing a long black dress, with white collar. I'm always too . . . I always have to behave and I don't want to – I want to laugh. I want to sing. I want to dance, like I did before, like I did with Mama."

"Are you in a room in the castle?"

"Yes, I can go to the entrance and then up the steps, one, two, three, four steps and then I'm in the big, big hall. Looks like it's made of marble and there are chandeliers. But it's very cold. I don't like it – it's much better outside in the warm sun."

"Can you go into one of the rooms and look in? Off the hall?"

"Yes, there is the dining room. There are more than twelve chairs – twenty-four chairs! All heavy-set chairs and chandeliers on the table."

"With candles?"

"Candles, many candles."

"Can you find the kitchen? Are you allowed to go in the kitchen."

"No."

"Have you ever snuck in the kitchen?"

"No. Because there is that, looks like a cook, he is in charge of the kitchen. With a black mustache, red cheeks, big heavy face, big, big man, big belly."

"He wouldn't let you see what's in there?"

"No!"

"Can you go upstairs to the bedroom?"

"I cannot go up the stairs."

"Is there a bathroom downstairs?"

"No. There is something that looks like a wooden tub – it looks like a barrel. And you put the water in, and you can put hot water in it."

"Big?"

"Yes. And there are pails to carry the water with. Yes. But why? That barrel doesn't fit with the marble."

"A barrel shaped tub made out of marble?"

"No. The floor is marble, and there is that funny wood-shaped – perhaps I don't know – tub."

"Is there a ground hall?"

"Yes."

"Is there a fireplace?"

"Yes."

"If you were allowed to, could you run in the fire place?"

"Yes."

"It's taller than you?"

"Yes."

"Is it cold in the castle?"

"Yes."

"Do you live there a long time?"

"Oh, I'm about twelve."

"Can you allow yourself to be older? Can you look at yourself older? Can you be sixteen or seventeen? Can you see yourself at seventeen?"

"Then I'm at the convent."

"You are at the convent, you are a novice."

"Yes."

"Can you hear?"

"I cannot hear anybody around me. There's no noise. It's so quiet!"

"You could hear the children playing in the tree when you were twelve? You told me children were laughing an singing when you were twelve. When you are seventeen, you cannot hear any noise."

"I cannot hear any noise."

"Something happened to you, Elisa. What happened to you? Were you hurt? Did you fall?"

"I think I fell down the stairs and that big cook with his mustache picked me up. I still don't like him. But he's very kind and he is a good cook. That barrel, that barrel is wine and it is not a tub. That is a barrel of wine. I know it now because he gave me something to wake me up and I did fall down the stairs. Ok. I feel fine again. I had fainted."

"But you cannot hear."

"But I cannot hear. I see them smile, but I cannot hear."

"Elisa, before you fell, when you were listening to the children and you were listening to your father and the big fat cook with the mustache, do you recognize what they're saying? Try to remember the children playing. Can you remember the children playing when you were climbing the tree, were they singing a song?"

"I cannot remember."

"Allow your mind to be very open and just try to get a word or two that was familiar to you then – it may not be familiar to you now. Allow your mind to be open. Try to form a word or two."

"Mama."

"Mama?"

"Mama, Joujou – that's the little dog."

"Now, Elisa, I want you to go back and rest. Back into the memory. And Erika, I want you to listen to me."

"I'm back in that coffin again. Why am I back in the little church?"

"Go back in the memory."

"In the church and then outside and in the graveyard, lying in the grave, they're closing it up."

"And now it can pass by. Now it can pass by and you return. I'm going to count slowly to three, Erika, and when I count to three, I want your eyes to open. Your body will feel very relaxed, you'll feel very comfortable about this experience that you've had, very calm and very comfortable. Your mind will be alert. Eyes will be open and you'll feel very relaxed and refreshed."

* * *

"Oh it's so frustrating," Erika says to Ruppert at home. "The session is always too short, and it seems to me that he cuts me off just when it gets interesting." They have both listened to the tape the psychiatrist made of her regression.

Ruppert shrugs his shoulders. "Time constraints. What can you do? That's the frame we live in."

Erika gives a dismissive wave, that slight movement that stops a breeze. "It's frustrating. It would have been incredible to find out just a little more, just another few moments. I see now he was trying to get at the language so he could place us in the world; I didn't understand that when he kept asking me for a word. I think my mind was on trying to figure out what made me die so young. Oh, I don't know."

"Don't be upset, it's no use. I can see how frustrating this is for you, but I think this is already pretty incredible, this window that's opened. It's giving you a sense of who you were at another time perhaps." He shrugs, tugs his head. "And, yes, it doesn't give you all the answers, but it provides a glimpse, a wonderful view that opens for just a moment. Not everyone gets that. And it gives you a chance to see something that's totally outside your life now, still, it's part of you somehow. How fascinating. Thank you for sharing this with me." He smiles warmly, then a sheepish glimmer glides into his eyes. "I have to admit, I'm sort of looking forward to your next session." He chuckles softly into himself.

"Me too," she says, and takes out the tape to date it. She then replaces a blank cassette into the slot before walking the recorder back to the nightstand in her bedroom.

CHAPTER 11

Love And Unfulfilled Promises

Erika enters the small examination room and greets the dark-haired, somewhat stocky fifteen-year-old who leans against the chair with eyes fixed on the floor. The teen's mother glares at Erika, scenting the room with stifled reprimands and silenced anxiety.

"Good morning," Erika says in cheery voice, holding the mother's gaze.

"Terry's been complaining that she's tired all the time and feeling sick to her stomach. I thought I'd better bring her in, in case she's caught a stomach bug," the mother says quickly, shooing a glance at her daughter.

Erika regards the teenager silently for just a moment, takes note of the soft lines of her face, remnants of open innocence fixed into unreadable mask. She's a child, really, sprung into the body of a young woman, the rift of a canyon slicing identity, this void in the yawn of growing up. "Well, let's see, shall we? Why don't you lie down here and I'll have a look at your abdomen."

"How long have you been feeling this way? Any vomiting?" Erika dives into routine questions as she feels her way around the teen's belly, and the girl just shakes her head. "Do you have a boyfriend? Any sexual activity?"

"No, uh-uh." Eyes sprung to life, darting to Mom. Erika's hands register the outlines of stomach, liver, spleen, uterus. She stops, retraces. Uterus? Above the naval?

No doubt, there it is.

"Let me draw some blood, and could you give me a urine sample? We'll run a few tests." She smiles softly at the teenager who avoids looking at anyone at all.

"What's the problem?" Mother's stern voice startles.

"When Terry's dressed, come into my office. Let's talk."

A few moments later, they've assembled. Mother sits across the desk, the girl slouches near the door, fidgeting with hands clenched quickly.

Erika meets Mother's gaze, then shifts to meet the teenager directly. Her eyes soften as she regards her, an embrace to catch a fall, and she takes another moment before splicing the curtain. "Well, we'll know for certain once the blood tests come back, but there's really no way to say this any differently. The analysis I just ran on your urine tells me you're pregnant."

A momentary pause and Terry's eyes widen, a deer caught on frozen road. She dashes them at her mother and back, a quick succession of flutters barely visible and heart-breaking. Mother has turned slowly, dread spread by her movement, and Erika knows she must continue still. Her voice drops to almost a whisper. "From the size of your uterus, I'd estimate about five months."

"Pregnant? What are you talking about? I thought you had the flu! You knew about this? You've been fooling around? Who is it?"

"No, Ma, I swear I haven't! I didn't!"

"Five months! You mean to tell me you didn't know? You had no idea when you didn't get your period? Are you kidding me? Five months? Five months. Wait a minute! You were visiting Aunt Becky around five months ago. Who got to you up there? Who?" Fear, dismay, anger all rolled into one. "Tell me! Tell me now! Who was it?"

"Please!" Erika interrupts quickly, her voice reining Mother into silence. "Please. I know this is very difficult for you, for *both* of you." She turns to Terry. "This news must come as a shock. Please know you're not alone with this, and you still have some options." She then turns to her mother, nods at her. "I know this is really hard to hear and even harder to accept because I'm sure you had different plans for your child. But, please hold off on any reprimands at the moment. From what I've just observed and understood, your daughter is as shocked as you. And more than anything, she needs your support, above all, she needs your support right now to get through this very difficult time." Erika pauses a moment, observes both in their silence, enmeshed in disquiet and unease, each trapped in her own disbelief. "I realize this is extremely difficult for you to accept, and this situation will need some time to digest, but it's happening, there's no doubt about that. More than anything, your daughter needs you to be there for her, she needs guidance and understanding." Her gaze sweeps to the girl, crumpled against the wall, and then to the mother. "She needs your support."

"Support? Understanding? *Understanding?* How can I understand that she's pregnant?"

"Please! Please understand that this is as much a shock to her as it is to you."

"She's fifteen years old! What's she going to do with a baby? What's she gonna do with this life?" Her frustration quickly turns to rage as she looks at her daughter, who's quieted so completely, a figure shrunken into smallness and disappearing into a trance within herself, unmoving.

"Exactly. She needs support, not anger. I understand you're very frustrated and angry right now, and as a mother, I really do understand your frustration perfectly, but please try to step back for just a moment and consider her for the moment. I know it is very difficult, but please, she needs you." She slows, faces the girl. "Terry, come sit here with us," pointing to the other chair. "Let's take a look at the options. At five months, the baby is coming. Now let's see what we can do once it gets here. Ok?" She looks into faces screwed tightly with pain, and reaches for her Rolodex. "For starters, I'm going to give you the phone number for a counseling group. They can offer advice and support to help you make a decision that's right for you."

As she writes down the information, the air has gone very still in the room. She knows she needs to try to soften this blow somehow for both of them, and turns toward them to discuss possibilities.

* * *

That evening, as she undresses, her eyes follow the thin line of the scar on her breast, and she trails it with her finger. Months ago, Ruppert had told her she's beautiful to him no matter what, but what about desire? The girl today, so youthful and young, and on a path she probably never imagined for herself. Erika startles, a wisp of air catching her breath at turns her life has taken so instantly, so unannounced. Part of her tugs yet another way, throwing worries and concerns and sapping her strength. She shuts the light in her room. *Let me sleep, just let me sleep.*

* * *

Gentle Reminders And Earthly Bonds

"I will help you receive knowledge from us within your boundaries of understanding. I am Joseph. With me is a group of friends, advisors, and teachers.

"Please don't ignore our messages because of earthly matters. They are too important for you, your family and others. You shall be our speaker because you have the energy and the courage to speak up for what you want. Over time, we will prove to you that we are as real as you, that only our composition is different, which you and your friends have yet to understand.

"Don't you feel the comfort of being yourself? And the security your material environment provides for your body, the extension of your soul? Don't you feel the warmth of your sheets, your covers and your pillow right now? And although we are past that stage of needing sexuality to preserve our race and are the complete form of both male and female part of the soul, bound together in one unit, we understand your feelings.

"Marriage has the same permanence as your physical surrounding and is a way of expressing comfort and security on Earth. It is the expression of two souls to be and stay together for the long journey they had jointly planned in a previous existence. It is a path of learning to give and receive for soul, mind and body.

"You lost that to some extent with Ruppert over the last few years. The feelings you lost lie especially in the physical expression of passion and intimacy.

"You and Ruppert spent several lifetimes together to learn physical passion with each other, in the way you loved each other soul to soul, as two energy sources in Interspace, which brought you peace, love and passion.

"When we told you that you still needed to learn the physical counterpart of this love, you wanted to try again. But, then as now, you failed to listen to your innermost need, and replaced your physical desire for each other with material fulfillment and wealth. And you're doing it again in this incarnation, reverting to your old life pattern of soul and mind unity instead of physical intimacy and passion. You are close friends with great respect for one another, but fail to achieve that closeness as lovers, too.

"You provide understanding, compassion and love to those who seek you out professionally, but fail to provide *each other* with the life energy you need to continue towards your goal of physical unity.

"Physical passion and unity attunes the vibration levels of soul and body. You lost that physical oneness in a previous life and have not been able to recapture it with each other in other incarnations entered for that purpose. Thus, you returned to planet Earth to try again.

"In achieving physical and emotional unity, you radiate positive energy patterns to other souls, especially those whom you serve as role models as they follow their own paths of learning.

"When two souls form a family, they freely radiate wholeness to other unattached souls, and reflect their success back to themselves. Recognizing their achievement, other single souls learn to acknowledge how love and peace are expressed in the physical form and understand the goal of returning to the source in love and peace. On the grand scale, the goal means to return to the eternal source, the Creator, in the infinite cycle of love, life and knowledge in acknowledgment of the very being itself.

"Both of you decided to remain in this lifeform despite several chances to move on. Each time, you resisted because you knew you had to complete this life together to fulfill your life cycle.

"Of course, there are many physical expressions of soul attunement, growth and acknowledgment. However, your goal lies in its passion and complete intimacy, and both of you, especially soul Ruppert, forgot yourself, your needs, goal and learning process. Professional service has taken its place.

"In fact, reaching that energy vibration of attunement mattered so much to Erika that she decided to continue her present incarnation although she recently had the chance to move on. But she decided to return so both of you can fulfill your chosen goal together. Both of you need this experience to continue your pathway of unity into the next dimension. She requires it for the completeness of her soul. Without it, she cannot return into other dimensions, nor can she grow sufficiently to complete the compound Olivia. She cannot fulfill her goal of patience, as you cannot fulfill yours of passion and love which you wanted to learn this time.

"Olivia? Help them accept their world's expression of soul, mind and body unity so they can fulfill their goal and Erika can return as the last learning experience of Olivia and thereby reach her destiny.

"Don't lose out, Olivia. I love you too much and want you back in my dimension so we can continue as one. There are unbelievable dimensions ahead of us. Without you I feel incomplete. I am your partner in your eternal goal and your helper and teacher for now. I will send you my strength and support. Love you, Joseph."

* * *

Erika shuts off the tape recorder and leans back against the pillows. Her eyes sweep to the clock. Almost 3 am.

Her thoughts trail across all the years her patients have taken precedence in her life. And it continues even now, when she hurries to the office and finds herself so exhausted by the end of the day that she can barely move once home. She closes her eyes, shrinks from what is true. Ruppert and she have become roommates with separate rooms for sleeping, which is all they do. *We bid each other good night and separate. Do we fill our days to the hilt to avoid each other? Can that be so?* She shakes her head. How she longs for him now, that togetherness they used to know. But how to get it back? It's been too long, hasn't it?

She thinks of their lives in Germany and on-call nights, when Ruppert would take the guest room to give her a break. Days turned to weeks turned to months, and then she couldn't stand his snoring anymore and asked him to continue to sleep there. Her shoulders slump as she remembers his eyes going very still and blending out, and she ignored it then because it's all she knew to do. Yes, it's her fault just as much. And now, well, most of the time, she's just not interested. Would he even consider it?

She heads to the kitchen for a glass of water, sees the light in Ruppert's room through the crack in the door and knocks.

"What are you doing up?" he asks, looking up from his book.

"A message came through and I can't sleep. It was about us and what we hoped to achieve in this lifetime and what we're in danger of losing. Oh Ruppert," she nudges her head into her shoulders, opens his door a little more, lets her eyes stray. "We're missing out with this not-sleeping together. I know we're both so used to it, and I can't even think of the last time we made love, but we're losing out. Joseph's message brought it to light for me, and it bothers me. I'm sad looking at it, but I have to say, he's right. Would you listen to the message?" She hears the pleading in her own voice, that tone of desperation that's slipped past.

Ruppert slides the glasses off his nose, sits up somberly and she knows he heard it too. "Of course," he says, pausing into stillness. "Do you have it now?"

"Yes, I can get it, that would be great. Yes. I'll listen with you again."

He follows her, sits down at the edge of her bed, quiets as her voice fills the room. When she clicks stop at the end, his gaze doesn't leave her.

"You know," he finally says, "I have to be honest with you. When you first came to me with the writing and then the first sessions, I was doubtful. Well, maybe not doubtful, but uncertain. I didn't know what all this was, I couldn't understand it. Tonight, however, he spoke to me, you spoke to me." He falls silent, his eyes searching hers. "I'm not sure where this will lead, if we can change any of our habits, but know that I love you very much, and, yes, he's right when he talks about our togetherness. We're one unit professionally, no doubt. And we confide in one another, but intimacy?" He shimmies his head into a tilt. "Well, that's gone, we seem to have lost that." He flickers a chuckle "Do you remember the night we got home and made love on the couch so long ago? Do you remember that passion we felt? God! We couldn't wait to be together." He slows. "What happened to us?"

She soaks up his rays, glances at her lap. "I know. And it seems we really wanted to do different, keep the passion, the love. Let's try to find it again." Their world slows, breathes on its own. And she senses herself with him on the sidelines.

"Who's Olivia?" he asks then.

"I'm not sure. I guess another part of me, maybe another lifetime." She listens into herself. "I get the sense she's a greater part of myself. I'd gotten the sense of a compound soul, maybe she's the one who collects all the experiences within herself? It all fills into her? I don't know. But it seems, my part strives to fuel her, maybe become her? Maybe she's wiser than me." Erika smiles at him.

"It's not Ophelia, then?"

"Ophelia, from Atlantis?" She shakes her head. "No, I don't think so. She's a separate entity from that. A different life, I think." She slows then, feels the moment passing. "Well, thank you for listening; it was important to me that you hear this."

"Ok. Let's talk tomorrow. Maybe we can figure out another way."

"I love you. Good night."

"You too." He smiles as she turns and pulls the door closed.

CHAPTER 12

Universal Origins

From her side of the couch, Erika watches Ruppert immersed in this month's finances, considering receipts before putting them aside. She scrunches her eyes and part of her falls away. Futile details? What's the point, really? Does it have any meaning in the entirety of the picture? And yet, so important in the now?

She breathes in deeply as a thought whispers tendrils to still her chaos. How many lives? Tens? Hundreds? More? Why this struggle? Birth, struggle, death, birth, struggle, death? Growing, studying, pushing forward, building comfort, overcoming disease, finding brief happiness, even love – for what? To do it again? Why?

"Ruppert, what's your thought on reincarnation?" She hovers a moment, waiting for a response. "I have to be honest, lately I find it daunting, this idea of never-ending existence, if that's what it is. What's the purpose of it all?"

He looks up from the papers before him, hands fanning out to mark a specific position. "Honey, please, not now. Let me finish this."

She turns into herself, struggles to stay aloft, pinpoints searching and flickering. Why do our spirits do it over and over? What's the point?

Joseph, are you there?

* * *

The Soul

March 25, 1989

"Good morning, Erika. Are you ready for a session?

"You wanted to know about the soul, especially your own.

"Souls are energy compounds of universal matter. All souls were created at the same time from an idea in the universal mind, called the almighty God in your world, who created them from the sparks of His own life force to fill the universe. Created in His likeness, they were meant to realize that they are similar but not identical to Him. He gave each a consciousness with which to understand all He showed them and sent them out to develop themselves. Each had the free will to choose its actions and follow its own path with the final goal of returning to the Creator and once again be part of Him.

"Each grew into the lifeform of its choice. All lifeforms had equal opportunities and possibilities to refine their life, and the same energy with which to fight, suffer, love, and hate. The souls were free to choose or reject emotions, which are part of the universal consciousness.

"Each had its goal, much like an explorer in your world. Their possibilities were almost endless and many materials needed to be formed. First, souls planned their surroundings in thought. Next, they designed a body, which is a wonderful but limited vehicle for learning, and takes into account that these souls cannot yet manage their infinite abilities as transpiritual[2] beings. Then, they created an environment in which to live and interact with other lifeforms. All this was done with the help of the Creator and according to His general plan. You were part of it.

"Some chose Earth, others selected other planets and other solar systems. Some chose to stay close to the Creator initially to observe. Others began to travel as energy forms, from solar system to solar system, from star to star. Each had the goal of returning to the Creator, the source of all life, hoping to have lived its life according to His wish and able to face Him.

"Many failed. Many did well. Those who succeeded tried to help those who could not overcome limitations they had created in themselves.

"This experience led to the formation of learning places to help souls form the goals that would make them similar, and eventually spiritually equivalent, to the Creator, and help them understand His will and recognize the many opportunities He gave them.

"As one of the learning places, Earth allows the soul to experience material situations and to develop its senses of touch, smell, hearing, well-being, peace and happiness. It was intended for those who wanted to experience life in human or humanoid

---

[2] Across, beyond, through – from what I gather, a spiritual being that crosses boundaries, is one with them and beyond them.

forms, or for those who were materially-oriented. However, throughout time, many souls were captivated by the material sense of happiness and its accompanying greed, power, struggle and terror. Thus, it has also become a place where souls learn to overcome hatred and terror which originated from a need for power certain souls were unable to control, which, in itself, upset the equilibrium within those souls and produced a negative behavior in form of hatred, fights, war, terror, and horror despite many opportunities to maintain love as their lifeform's foundation.

"All this was not in the initial plan of the Creator when He gave souls the freedom of development. However, although they acted against His will, their own free will allowed them to choose it as their path.

"Then as now, Earth is molded by the conscious everyday actions of its inhabitants' free will and thus experiences either times of spiritual evolvement or times of material development, although only spiritual growth is significant.

"To prevent continuous wrong-doing, a pause was introduced to the life cycle of souls on earth-like planets. This standstill allowed them to return to an 'inter-space' area and contact souls who had not diverted from their original plan and had become their teachers. They had halted their own advancement, as their own learning experience, to help return their brothers and sisters to the right path. It was there that we discussed your next life back to Earth.

"In Interspace, reincarnation to a particular planet is decided to help souls proceed towards their goals, since it provides a second, third, tenth, twentieth chance to reach certain stages of knowledge. After each incarnation, the souls return to Interspace to discuss their accomplishments with their teachers.

"Souls return to Earth knowing what they need to improve. With that knowledge, they form their reality in the physical to help them learn what they lack in their psychic and spiritual being. The soul chooses its fate on Earth according to its plan and may do so from its Akashic records[3]. However, once the decision is made, the information is sealed and the soul begins the journey of its new incarnation without conscious knowledge of its goal. While on the learning planet, it intuitively follows its plan.

"Once it reaches a certain level of development, a particular soul's yearning for spiritual knowledge may become so great that we once again allow it to look into its Akashic records and draw information in form of energy vibrations. The amount of knowledge received depends on the soul's urge to know. When the desire for spiritual knowledge becomes abundant, we, the teachers, are constantly nearby. If direct contact could provide the soul with an opportunity to higher learning, we open a channel of communication as a first step.

"You are one of our channels. Because you so much want to reach the Akashic records, we will give you a limited look into them. If you use the information to further your knowledge and share it with those we cannot reach, we would be helping you and you would follow your plan.

"You question your sudden ability to reach us and wonder if someone spiritually more advanced than you has somehow taken your place. The answer is no. You are the same soul; this is your second incarnation in one life. You have passed a stage of great suffering and desperation necessary to spiritually free your soul. In Interspace, we reviewed your life, including your profession, to prepare you for higher levels. We warned you of the hardships, but your strong feelings convinced us to give you the chance for a turning point.

"Your disease was necessary for your inner self. Many diseases will visit planet Earth to serve as learning tools for souls who are captivated by materialism. To recover their spiritual awareness, they need to complete the material stage of their learning and can do so only with the help of certain advanced souls and by suffering through an unexplained and unresearched

---

[3] A collection of all thoughts, actions, feelings, intent across all time, past, present and future

human disease. Since humans learn solely through the physical body, it has to suffer in its consciousness to free the soul or spiritual consciousness. Sometimes this is achieved only through fear, anxiety and pain. This is true of souls who, in their search for materialistic fulfillment, overlooked spiritual pleasure, which is expressed as happiness, peace and freedom and surpasses even the most exciting human physical pleasures.

"You, Erika, had to experience your disease so you can teach those who don't understand. You need to teach them that every cell has a consciousness, that the body consists of millions upon millions of cells and part consciousnesses. These make up your mind and soul consciousness and are directed by the spiritual consciousness of your soul.

"You need to teach others to be healthy spiritually, in mind and soul, because it is the soul and spirit consciousness that forms the body and creates the path for healing or destruction. Destruction occurs by way of diseases, healing by way of being well according to the physical and spiritual form chosen by the soul.

"The soul heals or destroys the body. As a unit, the souls of a generation heal or destroy generations. The souls of a race keep it in existence or destroy it. The consciousness of the whole human race will live in peace and happiness . . . or destroy itself.

"As a lifeform, the human race is on the verge of destruction. If this takes place, we can only contact those who are strong and advanced enough to start over with their gathered knowledge as colonists on a small undestroyed part of Earth or another world.

"Your goal is to be our speaker for peace and love, because only peace and love as brothers and sisters will keep you and your lifeform alive.

"We, from Interspace, will support and provide all our combined energy to those who listen to us. We will provide you with opportunities to speak about this to others until you return to us in preparation for your next learning experience.

"Good luck. Don't forget to enjoy life and earthly pleasures as long as you can. But don't forget your goal of which I will remind you in sessions like this.

"With love, Joseph."

* * *

Erika puts down her second cup of coffee. She had planned for an early-morning swim but got distracted, glued to this tape recorder, and is still sitting on the chair in her bathing suit when Ruppert walks in. She's just listened to it again.

"Morning," he says, pouring a cup of coffee. "What's this one about?" he asks, tipping his chin toward the recorder.

"Another session," she says, part of her still enthralled in this other world, this glimmer of vast existence, when his presence shifts her focus and she reemerges.

"When did it come in?"

"Early." She rewinds the tape again. "It's about the soul," she slows, holds tight. "I'm in awe," she finally says, and her body breathes relief. "I just listened to it again; I never went swimming. Is it too late?"

"You could do a quick dip," he says, glancing at the time, before nodding at her. She hovers another moment, decides then to take her chance and hands him the recorder before heading for the pool. He eases into the chair, puts down his coffee and presses play.

A few laps later, she opens the glass door. He looks up. "Where do you think it happened? Where did you start your second life?"

She wraps the towel around her, feet sliding drips onto the rug. When she sits down opposite him, she wipes at her feet with the edge of the towel, frowns. "I thought about that, too. Possibly the operation where they gave me all the fluids, especially since they kept evading giving a clear answer.

Remember, they simply said I needed more fluids. They never explained why." She lets it sink in. "Yes, that's what I think."

He tips his head, a stroke of wonder on his face. "Could be; that would explain it. My God, Erika." Startled eyes strike a pause in breath, embrace her as he shakes his head. "How could that be?" His hands reach up, swipe through his hair, clench tightly.

"Well, none of it, none of the anesthesia ever agreed with me." She hiccups softly into herself. "Look, it's done. It's over. I survived."

"Oh, Erika, thank God for that!" He stares at her and she can't read his expression. Suddenly she's aware of her wet bathing suit under the towel and she gets up just as the phone rings.

"Would you please get that?" she says as she heads to the bathroom.

He hesitates and lets it ring another moment before moving towards it. She listens for his words. "Iris, my dear," he says into the receiver, looks at her turn down the hall. "It's still going on? Hold on, she's right here."

"What's going on, Iris? Is it the court case? Is that still going on? Is that normal?"

"Nothing's normal, and I don't understand it either. Bill's mother talked us into using her friend and I wonder if it's a mistake. Granted, I don't know much about these proceedings and while he's not charging us much, I still wonder if we're in the right hands. The case has been referred to an Examiner, and they meet three days a month."

"Three days a month? For how long? For what? I thought the issues had long been decided."

"No, another got thrown in for good measure. The papers were an inch thick! I couldn't believe it. Bill's upset all the time and on edge," her voice trails off. "I'm sure you can imagine."

"How are you? How's all this affecting you?"

"I don't know. I'm nervous. I'm trying to ignore it, and am successful for the most part, but it's pretty upsetting. I've stopped going to these proceedings with him; he really doesn't want me upset, he's worried what it's doing to our relationship, our marriage. He may be right, I know it's affecting me, how could it not? And I'm sure that's what it's designed to do, but I'm in our marriage for the long haul, so we'll just push through this. It will have to end eventually. We all know it's not really the money that's at stake, it's a tool to hurt him and us, so it's not so easily settled."

A sigh into the silence, and Erika has heard the frustration in her daughter's voice. "I'm so sorry you're going through that. "Can I help in any way? Have you considered consulting with someone else?"

"Oh, Mom, it's not that easy. Bill's mother keeps reassuring us and the pressure's really high to keep him on. I can't really weigh in. It just keeps going on and on, and I really don't know what to do."

"How's Bill holding up?"

"Not so good. It's upsetting him. He puts on a good front, but I can hear him talk to himself when he doesn't know I'm near. He's angry all the time, understandably so. It's a struggle and there's no end in sight."

"Please let me know if there's anything we can do to help."

"There's nothing, Mom, it's running its course for now."

After Erika hangs up the phone, she finds Ruppert. "She's not telling me enough for me to give advice," she says. "And she's not listening. I know this man is not the right lawyer for them, not for this, but she won't hear me. She doesn't know what to do."

"Maybe it's not up to her," he says, turning to her. "You have to leave it be. Let her live her life. You can't interfere."

"How can they manage? They're both working stressful jobs, and this cloud keeps hanging over their heads. How can we help them? Isn't there a way to help them at all?"

* * *

Overcoming Negative Forces

May 25, 1989

"Give Iris love. Give the soul Iris all the support you can, spiritually and materially. She's forming a new life in herself, a lifeform that is also a part of you. It will be a boy she is carrying now, and he will look like her. I know this sounds incredible to you, but you'll see. He will be a strong, very manly boy with a bright future, both materially and spiritually, who will live in the spirit of the almighty Creator, upholding both their and your life ideas. You will be as proud of him as you are of her now.

"Her partner is a strong-willed man who helps her form herself while she continues on her path, which is united with his. Both came great distances to meet each other; it was their destiny. Having spent several happy and passionate lifetimes together, the most recent in the Far East, they were immediately attracted to one another and knew they needed to be together. They are part of the family and friends with whom you planned your present life.

"Their marriage is an expression of love overcoming negative forces. Like you, we will help them fulfill their goal. This will not be easy for them but both are strong-willed and their unit is stronger than any negative force trying to separate them. They went through a lot of hardship, which in itself made them strong and, knowing their goal and following the will of the Creator, they created their offspring at the right time as an expression of their unity and readiness to live according to their plan.

"They know that a family is inherent to any earthly plan. It is the foundation of tribes, communities, cities, countries and populations. It is a way to maintain the thought of love and peace, which transmits the vibration of peace to others and forms a conscious path through the various thoughts and approaches to religion, which exist only on planet Earth. Now, as parts of cultures, parts of the universal consciousness, they are giving parts of their souls to form and educate that lifeform within the will of their own Creator. They are an example of how humans in love can overcome spiritual, educational and cultural differences. Their existence serves as a small example to show the world the power of love.

"Support them without question and trust them the way they trust you; they are your own brother and sister souls. Give to them the way they gave to soul Erika in a previous life. Although they are younger than you in earthly time, their souls are as old as your own in infinite universal time, which is the composite of the many lives spent together within the same vibration level of love and understanding, while developing towards higher levels in the infinite universe.

"The success of their material ambition is a symbol of their unity despite their religious differences. It is a necessary expression of their souls to confirm what they already know: that a religion's name or way of celebration is not important in reaching the almighty natural force to be a part of the Creator; that each religion is merely a different way to approach and contact Him mentally and spiritually; and that a particular approach to religion is a small, very unimportant expression of love to and in the universal consciousness. Each advanced soul knows this, but less enlightened souls are too involved in materialism to realize it.

"If more people had their views, neither wars nor persecutions would have taken place because of religious differences thousands of years ago or now. If others cared for one another as they do, much bloodshed, pain and desperation could have been avoided.

"They see other souls and lifeforms on Earth as expressions of their thoughtforms and consciousnesses alone and know that love, the origin of their life, can overcome all differences. That point of view in more people could have prevented misconduct in many souls, many of whom were power-hungry, all of whom acted against the will of the almighty Creator.

"In the eyes of the Creator you are all one. You are parts of His creation, you stem from His thoughts, and are sparks of His consciousness. You are brothers and sisters. And although each of you is aware of your individual consciousness, *all of you are meant to work as a unit* to help one another on planet Earth according to your Creator's plan. Your final goal is to return to Him as individual consciousness, filled with your own learning experiences, and as a part of the soul consciousness that was given to you and which has been your guiding light.

"Try to see each lifeform as an expression of the almighty Creator. Although humans need leaders, only very few leaders have acknowledged the entire human race as an undivided spiritual unit with undivided growth as its goal. Many leaders are flawed and know only in their advanced soul consciousness that they are passing on false knowledge. Too many materialistic, power-hungry people elevated themselves into positions of spiritual leadership and became false prophets in the sense of the almighty universe. Still, most of them had a positive influence on the moral standards of their time. But forget all that. The goal of the almighty universe is to unite all souls with their individual experiences and eternal knowledge of goodness into a complete, itself infinite and ever-expanding consciousness.

"Think about it, Erika, and try to understand. Within the infinite dimensions of the universe, the lives on Earth make up a tiny component of learning to experience material ways, and are a vehicle to other dimensions with far more advanced lifeforms, who express their souls by listening to the sounds of the stars and feeling the vibrations of peace and love of the stars filled with advanced lifeforms united with each other in peace. It is a peace and equilibrium you can neither understand nor perceive with your present level of consciousness.

"We understand your urge to know, and want to answer your questions by opening your mind to this knowledge in a way you can comprehend. In turn, you need to teach others. Don't be afraid of ridicule. You can do it without harming your mission of healing, understanding, and love. Accept the challenge and start soon.

"That is it for today, in love and peace, your helper, Joseph."

* * *

My god. She's pregnant? And going through all this turmoil? Is that why she called today? She wanted to tell me? A cursory smile quickens her lips, startles.

She shuts off the tape recorder, takes it with her. "Ruppert? Where are you? Ruppert?" She finds him in the den. "You need to listen to this message that just came through."

CHAPTER 13

Religions And Other Differences

"How do you think they'll handle their differences?" Erika asks Ruppert as soon as the tape clicks to a stop. "Do you think they'll raise their child Catholic? Or would he not allow that?" She looks at him directly, watches for any reaction. "I know it's more important to you than to me, but raising the child Muslim? Is that a possibility?" A glide towards uncertainty, and somehow she's afraid.

"Well, I don't know, do I?" A curt answer through closed face, and the thread of pained hesitation lingers. "It's up to them. We've raised Iris Catholic, but she's reading the Koran and they both studied Arabic before their trip to Egypt in January. So, I don't know."

"I thought she might have converted. Didn't she? I thought for sure she did."

"Didn't you ask her?"

"Every time I open my mouth, we argue. I can't do it anymore, I'm afraid to broach the subject."

"So you've just decided on an answer. Well, you know as much as I." He turns to gather yesterday's mail. "Maybe we should just wait and see. Of course, you could always ask Joseph."

A moment's hope flickers across her eyes and she nods as from far away. "Yes, yes, I'll do that. I'll do just that."

* * *

"Ruppert, a message came through this morning, early! Come, let's listen together, can we?" Erika has hurried into the kitchen, recorder in hand, excitement flushing her face. "If we hurry we can do it before we need to leave for the office."

He turns from the coffee machine, fills two cups. "Sure. Put it on."

She's placed the recorder on the counter between them and presses play as they both settle in to listen.

* * *

Religions In The World

May 27, 1989

"Here is Joseph. You wanted to know about the many religions in the world today.

"They are all parts of one belief, of one God: the real and only God in your sense, the Creator of the unified universe as He was and always will be.

"You reach God when you pray, meditate, try to find explanations to all the unanswered universal questions in your mind and soul, and when your mind quiets to try to unite with the universal consciousness and the vibration of love and peace, which your soul expresses as patience and love.

"The knowledge of universal forces was sent to unify the people and guide them throughout their experiences towards their acknowledgment of God, the almighty Creator of the infinite and ever-expanding universe. By way of the universal consciousness, the messages were meant to explain the soul's infinity in the cycle of life: that each soul is a lifeform, infinite in its existence and united with the whole in the cycle of life within the infinite universe. The individual, as well as all souls as a unit, expresses this truth by acknowledging the knowledge it gained during the experiences of its learning process to become, itself, a mirror picture of the almighty Creator. God gave each spark the gift of free will, including the choice to accept or refuse His ideology."

"Although various ways of help exist for a soul that has embarked on its path of knowledge, cultural nuances or ethnic differences make it sometimes difficult to interpret or understand the teachings or the universal forces. That is because the information was always tailored to a specific people living at a particular time in a specific place, so that each, in its particular state of life, could understand them. Thus, when the more advanced in a culture tried to interpret the knowledge because they had become aware of an overall mission of the souls, they interjected their own momentary state of consciousness into their interpretation and involuntarily changed the meaning of the information, resulting in different ways of worshipping on Earth. They failed to attune to their knowledge within, and thereby failed in their mission to correctly impart their knowledge of the ideology.

"All souls were striving to reach the next higher state of their lifeform, that of love and peace. They knew that these are the creative forces of energy in any lifeform that keep it alive by preserving its life energy or consciousness. It is these creative forces that keep the universe together according to universal laws and in the sense of universal balance. Only the creative force maintains the equilibrium in the atom, so it can, with other atoms, form the molecular system. It, in turn, maintains the balance in the molecular system to keep all the organs in balance, which keeps the entire lifeform in its vibrational and energy balance.

"However, they were unable to reach this spiritual level of the creative forces. Instead, they were ever more drawn to the material side of their lifeform: their body, and all its accompanying material expressions, until they reached the lowest vibration levels on Earth. As they drew closer to the material side, they still acknowledged a higher consciousness and therefore developed various social hierarchies of ideologies, naming them religions. As part of their voluntary learning process, they were sent to the world again and again to complete different stages of their spiritual development, each time as a different image of their Creator. For each incarnation, each soul adjusted and attuned itself to its momentary lifeform with its particular conscious state to again acknowledge the vibration form of love and peace as it was meant to be.

"Souls who were attuned to the lowest vibration levels of the material lifeform forgot this as they embraced that level's expression of enjoyment and happiness. Their goal had been to learn about matter and gravity by experiencing this vibration level, but they forgot the purpose of their mission while experiencing sensual and purely material happiness. Their need for joy became so powerful that they took by force what they could not attain in peace and patience. By doing so, they voluntarily attuned themselves to negative forces of power, violence and terror. Thus, an initially positive ideology of learning became a negative expression, voluntarily chosen, and created negative vibrations within that lifeform itself.

"Since this has occurred many times throughout millenniums, several attuned souls were sent to the world to be acknowledged as mirror pictures of the Creator, and as the ideal of the soul each spark was meant to be. Among them were Buddha, Confucius, Mohammed, Christ and Adam. In trust and patience, they all acknowledge the vibrations of love and peace as the compounds of their wholeness. They were sent to Earth to remind the lost souls what had been meant for them and what they can achieve by acknowledging and attuning themselves to the truth within: that they could reach equilibrium within their soul and oneness with all by worshipping the Creator and resuming their life according to the law of lifeform. They were shown this with the chance to acknowledge as much of it as their momentary state of life and awareness was able.

"This knowledge gave each the opportunity to continue on its intended path within the vibrations of love and peace with the goal to reach higher levels of consciousness, away from the material-oriented consciousness of the body. They could do this by attuning to the infinity of the soul, which is the composite of the learning experiences at various learning places in the universe, with diverse levels of acknowledgment and attunement to different vibrations and learning dimensions. All souls pass through these learning stages to reach their goal of returning to eternity as part of eternity itself, to achieve wholeness as part of the wholeness of all souls, and to attain in its soul consciousness the entirety of the Creator's ideology.

"Olivia, you learned this during several reincarnations on learning place Earth. You are the composite of that knowledge on its way to fulfillment to the next dimension. You will reach it if the last incarnation Erika follows her plan and attunes herself with you, Olivia, to fulfill her learning process of love and peace in trust and in patience.

"To reach her goal, Erika interacts with those she and her soul partners planned to share experiences and learning during this reincarnation, having all voluntarily chosen to help each other in love and peace, and acknowledging their combined goal. This may also liberate your souls for higher dimensions with new learning processes, goals, achievements, attunement and acknowledgment for oneness toward your acknowledged goal.

"There is only one God, one Creator of creative lifeform, of creative life force. He brought the sparks of His consciousness to life as souls for the chance of voluntary learning and achievement. He gave them the opportunity to become mirror pictures of Himself through experiences and learning processes on different dimensional levels . . ."

The tape recorder clicks a loud stop, abruptly splicing the flow of sounds, and startling everyone in the room. Erika looks at the recorder, presses play against resistance, hoping it's just a snag. But it refuses to catch, and just won't continue. Ruppert takes it from her, opens the compartment to retrieve the tape, and she folds within. The tape has come to its end.

"No, that's no good. You've run out of space on the cassette." He turns to her with raised eyebrows.

Her face fallen, crescent moons focus on his hands. "Oh, Ruppert! Just when it was getting interesting. How could this happen?"

"It's only a 60-minute tape and I guess you added to your last session? Do you not take a new cassette for each one?" He waits for her to answer, stops himself from prodding further when he catches her expression. "I'll get the 90- or 120-minute tapes.

That's too bad, really, but no need to fret. You'll do it differently from now. I'll get some today. I promise."

She's clenched her hands, swipes at the countertop, clicks her tongue. "Oh, Ruppert, really, I can't believe it. I can't believe I did that. It's gone, it's gone, I've lost it all. All the things he said after that, I don't even know what it was. It's all gone, Ruppert. I've lost it." She turns to face him, a form suddenly crumpled within herself. "I can't believe it. I lost it."

He wraps his arms around her, pulls her close. "Oh, hon, I know it's disappointing, but please don't upset yourself more. There's a lot of information here. The gist of it is all there, I'm sure." He focuses on darkened eyes. "And, hey, what if you ask the question again? Maybe he can tell you again what's missing? I'd imagine he might repeat what we need to know?"

She looks at him, twists out of his embrace. "I have to get ready for the office," she breathes a jagged exclamation, her chest aflame as she walks down the hallway.

CHAPTER 14

The Search For Truth

May 29, 1989

"Good morning, Erika. Look into the mirror. What do you see?"

Her eyes scan the wall and see the reflection. "A cross with Christ on it."

"It is the mirror's reflection of the cross on your wall. Just as I am a reflection, an image and part of the reflection of Christ. The way I, you, and Christ are part of, and an image of the

Creator of the universe. As were Buddha and Confucius before, when they came to your world to influence the human race in its momentary state of consciousness towards acknowledging and accepting the ideology of the Creator.

"Each had followers and enemies. Those who followed them in faith and trust entered a realm of peace and love in their soul. They radiated their faith into their surrounding by expressing their beliefs of peace and love.

"The religions of your world are reflections of the same idea that was brought to different groups of people at different times. In our realm, we are part of the same idea: we want to teach you the same laws of love and peace in your dimension so you, with the help of others, can preserve the equilibrium in your planet, your galaxy, and, finally, in our entire universe.

"I am Joseph. I am part of the vibration of love as it was in its creation: a part of the Creator. You are also meant to be a part of that vibration as its mirror picture. So were Adam and Eve. They were meant to live in their vibration dimension called Eden, however, they did not understand that they were an image and a part of the almighty being, not him. When they started to believe they were almightier than He, they rebelled against their own beings and lost contact with the high vibration level of their origin. But they were not abandoned. Instead, they were given a chance to learn to free themselves of unnecessary needs for material structure and power. To do so, they lived in dimensions of lower vibration levels to prepare themselves to live in the ideal, highly-developed, unbelievable dimension of the vibration of love, which itself is a mirror picture of the Creator and close to Him.

"Since then, souls have returned to learning place Earth and will continue to do so until they are ready in their consciousness to travel freely to other dimensions and realms, which are learning stations to raise awareness of the oneness of us all as part of the consciousness of the Creator of the universe.

"Look at the cross again, Erika, what do you see?"

"The reincarnation of Adam, who returned and, as an expression of love, took all his experiences and those of all humans and the world into his consciousness, and returned them as a gift to his Father. In turn, the Creator's gift to him and the world is, through unity, transformation into the almighty creation itself."

"That path is your destiny as it is for all humans. You will continue on it repeatedly until you reach, in peace, the knowledge and understanding in your consciousness. And until it is part of every part consciousness of your lifeform, meaning in the very consciousness of your atoms and molecular structures all the way to the lifeform itself.

"Look back at the cross as the truth of the world and as the reflection of the love the Creator has offered your world by giving you His son as an expression of his own consciousness, in trust and faith. Just as he sent the sparks of his consciousness in trust to acquire the soul experiences needed to acknowledge the truth and the peace of His almighty consciousness.

"Truth and faith are the everlasting truth in the eternal expression of love. Truth is an energy form of feelings experienced by souls vibrating in the same pattern, who search for the same knowledge and acknowledge the same paths in their search for the truth. Dare to see the incredible, wonderful, and breathtaking dimensions with all their lifeforms, the consciousnesses, the vibration and energy forms interacting in their endless search for the truth, the only real truth that is love and peace and faith.

"That is and was the truth from the very beginning. Materialism and greed buried it, yet some souls rediscovered it. But they are too few to realign the world on its path of eternal life, or to re-establish the peaceful alliance with other galaxies and stars in other dimensions in the eternity of the universal laws of balance.

"In acknowledging the law of the universal balance and the forces that maintain the equilibrium within the universe, souls launched religions. However, they were created as matter, as thoughtforms brought to life by material lifeforms who had descended to the lowest level of vibration. And as matter, the religions themselves were worshipped by human beings, instead of being an expression of truth to find the Creator.

"The souls tried to maintain a positive direction within their consciousness, however, their originally well-intended creations misled others and the entire cycle of life into even lower vibration levels, on a negative course into the levels of pure materialism of temptation and pleasure, which were misinterpreted as fulfillment.

"Thus, souls of high vibrational levels became trapped in low vibration patterns and adapted to them. Unable to free themselves, they eventually forgot the ideology of the Creation. Their souls returned again and again to these low vibrational levels and the gravity of planet Earth. They did this in an attempt to rediscover themselves, their high vibrational pattern and their goal to search for the truth in the hope to liberate their souls from the material thought and action. Success would allow them to live in the material vibrational pattern of gravity as a learning tool and project only, as it was meant to be, not for eternity, as misguided souls interpreted it.

"When the Creator developed the souls and gave them the opportunities to develop themselves with the free will to follow or reject His plan, most of them concurred. However, some rebelled. You remember the event as the revolution of Lucifer, the Bearer of Light, who revolted against the Creator, thinking he was His equal. He was created in His image and could create light like the Creator, but Lucifer did not acknowledge that he was a mere mirror picture of the Creator and not He. Just like Adam.

"Now, the human race follows in their steps. They think they are like the Creator because they can create life, atoms and molecules, and destroy life, in its beginning and its spirit. They also think that this ability to destroy or split atoms gives them the ability to rule the world. They do not realize it will ultimately terrorize and destroy the world.

"There is a fine line between creating life, which is the truth and the real Creation, and destroying life in distrust and death in its eternity and complete negative force.

"The truth is the truth. There are no other answers. It is the only truth possible in any lifeform independent of time and space. A lifeform wanting to grow by searching for truth itself needs to merely acknowledge it: the truth of love, of acknowledgement of the Creation, and of the consciousness of the Creation in the sense of creating.

"Search for the truth. That is your goal and your path to eternity. It is this truth you are striving to find during your last incarnation, in hope that your soul will survive as Olivia. Only by returning to your path will you find your way to the Creator, as a part consciousness of the universal consciousness, as it was meant to be. Go forward and don't look back. Love you, my love, Joseph."

* * *

"Hey, would you look at that, he answered your question," Ruppert says to her with smiling eyes after the tape has come to its end. "This must have been what he said to you before." He slows. "That's extraordinary."

Erika smiles back at him, the glint of relief and satisfaction sweeping across her sight. "It does give me more insight. But I have to admit, I'll have to listen to it again to get it all in. It seems so complex to me." She turns thoughtfully. "Well, maybe not so much, maybe it's really very simple. And I'm really glad for the insight. Although that doesn't answer my question as to how Iris and Bill will handle religion with their child."

"Maybe it's not our business to know. Maybe they haven't even discussed it yet. Let them figure it out. Give them time. Give them a chance to do it on their own." He slows, then tilts his head ever so slightly. "Has she told you she's pregnant yet?"

“No. I haven’t spoken to her since the other night.” She falls quiet, murmurs, “I don’t know how to.” The whispers cast a shadow in her eyes.

“Well, give her a call. You’ll see, it’ll be ok.”

She’s retreated. “I’ll do it tonight.”

“Don’t put it off too long,” he says softly, leaves it at that.

She steps away, her mind filled with the conflicts of her soul, speaking loudly into her ear and she’s not ready to hear.

CHAPTER 15

The Law Of Trust

June 3, 1989

Good morning, Erika. It's five a.m. Today, let's talk about the law of trust.

"Trust is the precious vibration of giving and receiving that should be treasured by humans. It is the interaction of two souls vibrating in the same pattern when they intuitively know the truth. This truth cannot be altered by the mind, whether logical, evil, materialistic or power hungry.

However, the vibrations of truth and trust can be negatively affected by logic, even if positively intended. Once manipulated, even towards the 'right' direction or the positive path of trust, the vibrations take on negative qualities which destroy positive energy and the vibrations of goodwill, as well as the authenticity of trust itself.

"Only genuine trust stirs your soul. It occurs when soul energy is given and received as it is meant to be. When building friendships with trust, you need to choose carefully, selecting souls with whom you had contact in earlier times. You cannot find them with logic, but need to seek them out with your heart. Remember, trust is the particular vibration pattern shared by two souls at the moment they know the truth, no matter what its vibration level in your material world.

"Souls are finite compounds within the infinite universe. They are made up of vibrating particles that are attracted to them the way the solar system attracts and forms its planets from particles of the universe.

"Souls are the vibration sparks of the ever-loving Creator. They used the energy of the universe to form themselves into minute mirror pictures of Him and created their own material surrounding through vibrations, which included bodies and their accompanying living environment. Each of those forms has its own unique vibration and density, as has Earth's matter and gravity, to which you have become accustomed, to learn what it means to live in these elements.

"The body is the soul's expression of physical matter and has a particular vibration. The mind interacts between soul and body. Sometimes the mind is blinded by its attraction to physical matter and can no longer sense the higher vibration of the soul, which is sometimes reflected in man's inability to hear higher frequencies. He lost contact with them as he accustomed himself to the lower frequencies of matter and its vibration pattern, which is the lowest on the entire scale.

"The soul, however, remembers the highest, most translucent frequencies of its origin and creative energy as its expression of living. It remembers vibration patterns of translucent matter in other dimensions, where matter in the sense of material substance is not important, and where souls form and transform themselves into translucent lifeforms, creating translucent environments. There, souls form and transform colors, sounds and forms as expressions of their own vibration in an ever-changing vibration pattern of waves in moments of time units that are comparable to yours.

"Our timeframe is infinite, as is the process of change we all undergo. The continuum of change includes the planets as they circle around the sun, and the atoms and molecules as they travel around the nucleus of the cell. It includes interstellar systems and constellations that form and transform energy waves, thereby creating lifeforms that contain the growing consciousnesses meant to evolve to greater and higher awareness. All this is done in trust and moves towards the goal of creation: evolvement and transformation of the lifeform as it was meant to be. It all occurs in one unit of time.

"Time is infinite, no matter how it is observed. You are part of the infinite plan and, according to it, you change, ever learning, experiencing and evolving. One of your goals now is to find and learn to trust.

"Did that answer your question? Love you, Olivia. Joseph."

* * *

She knows she has to call her daughter, the urgency a splinter under her skin nudging her again. *Why do I find this so difficult?* Already, a murmur sweeps over her, the drag on the ocean floor. Still, she picks up the phone, dials, hears it ring, one, two, three into the recording. Part of her breathes easy at the sound. "Hey, it's Mama. Call me when you get in? I love you."

CHAPTER 16

Unity

June 5, 1989

Erika, you want to know about Bill and Iris' future. It is a very bright future because they love each other so much and are meant for each other, as I already told you.

"To you, it looks as though they're still struggling, but look at their radiating eyes, recognize their unity, their feelings and love for each other, which is intense and unified, and different from last year or the year before. They have melded in mind, spirit and body. Iris melded into Bill's soul and that is their destiny. She senses it and is happy about being part of his soul.

"They will continue along their path intuitively, in a knowing from previous lives and experience. Therefore, understand and help them if they need any interim material help and they will return it by way of grateful thinking and awareness, especially Bill, in appreciation of your support and understanding of two different religious worlds. They will be successful and won't need much financial assistance, only reassurance, confidence, and acknowledgment of their unity as their destiny, which they already know since they authored it.

"Of course, it will be a boy she is carrying now. He will have light hair and will resemble Iris with his very strong will, soul and spirit power. He will get the name Joseph, because he is Joseph. I will lead him in awareness of the universe and the almighty Creator, and in our sense of giving. He will be raised a Muslim – what does it matter, you all believe in the same Creator of the universe. It is merely a different form of worshipping the same God you all believe in.

"Give them understanding and reassurance, especially to her. Let Iris know that you understand her current religious belief is the same path to the same almighty Creator of the universe. This is important to express now, rather than at a future time. Make it clear that you are part of them, trusting and believing in them and their future, otherwise Iris will become distant again, as mistrust returns and causes you to feel you're losing your daughter.

"Share their belief in themselves, their gladness, joy and trust, and acknowledge their united pathway. See them as a unit towards their destiny which they chose with you in Interspace, where you already knew about your balanced fate and destiny even if it was not always easy. Remember, planet Earth is your learning experience and you all have learned pretty well, while remaining together on your chosen path.

"Love is a very strong force. It gets our attention over here because it touches our realm. We readily provide understanding and awareness to anyone on the right path, to increase their awareness and keep them on track. I will always give you the best advice I can, bringing success to you and anyone who will listen.

"You were my professional friend, my friend, my partner, and my love in several life times, especially as Olivia. Even now, as part of the compound of Olivia, you are Olivia to me. I love you, Joseph."

* * *

Erika can feel Ruppert's eyes on her while the tape replays. For a moment, she glimpses a reaction flicker in his face, reflecting recognition of this truth and his momentary struggle to believe it, the uncertainty, then the acceptance, shifting his body into calm. He slides the glasses higher on his nose, looks at her reluctantly.

"Can this be true?" The air has gone out of the room in the moment's stillness, that rare instant when all is and nothing remains on a single breath.

A thin line tugs at her cheeks, slides into her eyes. "Grows on you, doesn't it?" She tips her chin at him. "Sure does with me. I wonder. I truly wonder. I'm afraid to ask her now."

"Well this is the last thing that should stop you. It should inspire you to find out! Hey, I'm dying to know, I want to know now what's going on. If you don't call her, I will. I'm done waiting."

"Alright, alright, hand me the phone. I'll do it right now. Right now." She points with her eyes, dials the number, draws up her eyebrows as she listens to the ringing.

Then, she turns toward the phone, speaks confidingly, "Hey, it's me. How are you?"

A slow grin slides into Ruppert's face as he turns to leave to give her some space.

"I'm fine, Mama, really. How are *you?* How are you feeling?" Iris chirps into her ear.

For a moment, Erika isn't sure what she means. "Oh that, I'm fine. I'm good, healthy, no problems. What's going on with you?" She resists the urge to speak about the court case. Today she promised herself to step back and let Iris talk, and she lets the silence stretch a little longer.

"Mom, I have something to tell you," she says, and Erika finds she's holding her breath as this tingle of joy sidles into her heart.

"Yes?"

"You're going to be a grandmother. I'm pregnant."

"How wonderful!" The lift roars her heart, still somehow unexpected, quiets to a murmur within her core. "Ruppert! Ruppert come here! Iris is pregnant. How far along are you? How are you feeling?"

"Just about seven weeks . . ."

"Wonderful, just wonderful. Isn't that something. Any morning sickness? Cravings? Can I send you something?"

"I'm alright, Ma. Mornings aren't too good, but unsalted Saltines before I lift my head off the pillow do the trick. It's not too bad, really, and, well, I'm just so excited!"

Erika's face has become pure rapturous delight as she presses her ear against the phone. "I'm so thrilled for you."

"Thanks Ma."

"You're still working?"

"Oh yes, no change there yet. I haven't told anyone the news, we want to wait until the three months are up before telling anybody. You're the first one who knows."

"I'm sure the baby'll be healthy. Have you thought about what you'll do after? Will you go back to work?"

"No, Mom. Bill and I've discussed this at great lengths. I'm planning to stay home with the baby. It's better in the long run. If I'm going to be a mom, I'm going to be a Mom!"

"Well this is just wonderful news. I'm so glad. I love you, honey."

"Love you too. I've got to go, I'll keep in touch."

Erika snugs the phone, waves it in the air. "Ha! She's going to have a baby! Joseph was right. My little girl is having a baby!"

Ruppert has stopped moving, and stands there in momentary stillness of joy, tugs his head slowly back and forth. "She's having a baby." His eyes glint. "Joseph called it right."

She slows for the moment. "I'm relieved," she says, notes the question in his eyes. "Because if he was wrong, then it would question these sessions, and, I suppose, my sanity in a way. So, I'm really glad. And I'm relieved that I'm hearing right. I mean, I'm picking up on images, sensing pictures, and interpret them, and I often wonder how much I'm distorting with wishful thinking what I actually perceive. It's so quiet and all, like that small still voice within that's so easily ignored. And here, I try to hone in on it and get it right. And I never do know for sure, you know? I mean, I can't just ask him, or you can't just ask him to verify, can you? It all goes on inside my own head, and, who knows? But I'm glad I got this right." She smiles again. "I'm really glad."

"Well, I've always believed in you. And even if you ever miss on the details, I don't think it really matters in the long run, not with the whole picture. And, well, I wonder how much is cast in stone, when you think about free will. I know he said that it's a boy with blond hair who will be raised Muslim. But does that really matter? Would we love him any less if he turned out to be a girl with brown or red hair? It wouldn't matter one stitch, doesn't matter at all. So, even if he's raised Muslim, as he says, it doesn't matter. It's foreign to us, but as long as they teach him a belief in God, what difference does it make? And anyway, maybe they haven't really made up their minds yet at all, maybe they're still considering their options. Who are we to tell?"

"I suppose you're right. And me, myself," she snorts gently, "I don't go to church every Sunday, we both know that. In fact, I think I'm keeping *you* from going more than you are, and I'm sorry I have that influence on you if that's the case." She has turned to him, her face open and reminiscent of their early years together. "I get wrapped up in myself and my work. I'm sorry."

"Don't worry, I make my choices, too. And we have to let them make theirs. We have to remember to keep back and let them make their own decisions, their own lives. We owe them that."

"I suppose you're right. It's hard, though, especially now again." A wistful smile beckons her lips. "It's hard. I'll try."

CHAPTER 17

Nagging Doubts

"Have you told Iris or Stephen about these sessions with Joseph?"

She has slowed at the question, so seemingly innocent on the surface. "No," she says, through shadow resting in her breath.

"Will you?"

She's picked up on his laid-back tone that scrapes along an artificial glimmer, and something grating stands up inside her. *What is the matter with me?* Without answering, she searches his face for suspended sound. And, within herself, she senses mother hen deliberately corralling her chicks within reach. "I haven't given it any thought." It pains her to approach this nagging space within her. "I don't know," she says then, a fleeting whisper. "Please don't push me. I've already shared my cancer with them; I don't know what to do with this. I need some time."

He looks at her, the corners of his eyes softening. "Ok." He tilts his gaze, pauses. "I just wanted you to give it some thought; it's so important to you that you might want to share it at some point. There's a real gift of information here, I don't think you want to just keep that to yourself, or us."

"I don't think I'm ready to do that. What would they think of me? What would anyone think if it got out? The crazy woman doctor who lost her mind after breast cancer?" She shakes her head quickly, a rugged jerk. "No. Please, just leave it alone for now. Please." She turns toward the collection of vitamins on the counter, searches through the labels as she slides them out of the way, one by one.

He watches her for another moment. "Maybe you could just tell them what happened to you. Let them listen to a tape. You know Iris is interested in spiritual things; she's been searching just like you. She'd understand, for sure."

She glides the bottle an inch at a time, senses the clamp tightening around her. "It's too personal," is all she can manage. "I'm not ready." She frees the vitamin from its dark cave, chases it with water. "Please leave it for now, just leave it."

"Alright then," he says, taps the counter once with his finger, shrugs. "It's a beautiful sight. You ought to let them in."

Weary tide engulfs her and she breathes into the ominous fog, trying to unblock the peculiar tightness his words have created within her, moves through the maze and pours herself a cup of coffee.

*   *   *

Just Believe

June 15, 1989

"Why are you so worried about losing the messages? You know they are recorded in the Akashic records and you can call on them at any time. Don't be afraid. Believe in yourself, and believe in us, who are teachers for your spiritual and soul growth. Only your growing awareness is truly important.

"In your world, war and incredible famine always exist somewhere, just as overwhelming surplus and unbelievable wealth and joy reign elsewhere. These extremes destroy the balance of peace planned for Earth and intended for the many generations of Adam and Eve's children.

"Adam and Eve's mistakes hindered the progress of all people. And although we tried to influence man for millions of years, we have not been able to show him the flaws of his development. We have yet to convince man of his self-imposed limitations of using only a very small part of his available knowledge, feelings, and senses to arrive at pleasure. Man's way does not unify him with the almighty Creator, nor does it give him all the joy and peace waiting for him in the form of Eden on planet Earth, according to the plan.

"Jesus Christ and Noah have tried to influence man, as have several unknown and lesser-known people of varied professions, who were meant to show contact with their Akashic records by demonstrating fantastic abilities they could not have learned on their own. They included Michelangelo, Alexander the Great, Rembrandt, Mozart, Beethoven and Bach. One of the last was Einstein.

"Evidence of this exceptional and one-of-a-kind talent in any of your vocations was intended to introduce the idea of beings in higher dimensions. So were sightings of UFO's. You always wondered why we chose regular people, the common person, rather than public figures, celebrities or the like, to contact and report sightings of UFO's. We thought that the average person could reach acceptance of others more readily. Unfortunately, our signs were dismissed as peculiarities, as was Einstein's theory of time, which reached limited acceptance within certain groups but not in the mainstream of society.

"Consider this: to understand and see a person's complete life span, you must first accept the fact that you live *simultaneously* in the past, present and future. Time units are all part of one time link, interactive and interwoven within the memory chambers of your brain, which you can access once you have the keyword. Mozart had the keyword for music as a child. That is why notes streamed forth from his mind and formed to songs and incredible compositions, incredible for his time. Unfortunately, then as now, they were accepted as entertainment only, not as part of the universe and the almighty God as they were meant to be.

"To this day, his compositions are played all over the world. But you listen to them in an earthly sense alone and as a past you think is gone. That past is your future, too. Once you are mature enough, you will reach dimensions which have recorded the cause of Mozart's ability. And you will see, feel and hear the abundant compositions of a world of stars. You will realize that music is the sounds of joy, the love and interactions of stars, and millions of vibration sounds of the cosmos.

"El Greco received a glimpse of a world in another galaxy that was populated by a people whose expressions and lifeforms were transmitted to him in an instant. He was fascinated by them and their idea and translated those lifeforms onto his paintings. Since he painted them, these lifeforms have evolved much further and have filled galaxies. You would not be able to recognize them, except for their outer form. Their inner form was not captured quite accurately in the pictures and has developed to an almost completely lucent and thoughtform-like state.

“The little children of Lourdes received a glimpse into the Akashic records from us, which told them of a future event, a sign in the sky, a fireball, to warn humanity to change and avert from the hatred and terror, which negatively formed your atomic knowledge. That fireball will be an accidental explosion of atomic power which will harm many of you, but return others to the faith they had lost.

“With that in mind, seeing what you are missing and where you unknowingly made mistakes, you return to learning place Earth to start all over again. Once you reach a certain level of understanding, you no longer return. Instead, you travel to a planet for spiritual development in another dimension and towards another dimension of your consciousness. You are presently in a phase where you are receiving understanding. Up until now, you have not received actual knowledge but a glimpse of understanding and awareness of the existing possibilities.

“We will give you, piece by piece, knowledge on how to reach those states, as your yearning grows in your inner self. Your inner feelings know the truth. Don't let logic hold you back.

“Your inner feelings are your contact to us and the way we reach you. And now, by listening to yourself and placing higher importance on your inner feelings, you can call us. Weave this into your daily life's importance. It should be as important as silver threads woven into a cloth. The more silver threads you weave the more valuable the time you spend on this will become.

“Faith, love, trust. You have to learn indefinitely, knowing that these feelings are the path to your future which has already begun and which was your past. It is the knowledge you always received when you returned to Interspace to learn and to compose your future life with us, as future lives are composed and laid out in a rough blueprint. You will learn, as will loved ones, who have to complete their own path of learning, at their own speed, using their own choices. But they are around you, as they were in the past and will be in the future, interwoven like stars in the sky above you on a quiet, calm and clear night.

"Love you, Joseph."

*   *   *

"What a fantastic place, fantastic idea to bring a child into," Erika whispers after the tape has clicked to a stop, looking out the window with a look of innocent wonder, gets up quickly to find Ruppert.

"This is amazing," she calls to him, jutting the recorder at him. "You have to listen to this; what an incredible idea, this chance to grow, to learn, another chance for another step towards completion. Too bad we can't just take some of that knowledge with us, consciously. Maybe then, our existence, all of humanity would take better care of this planet, of our Earth and its resources, of each other, of some of the indigenous people, cherish what knowledge they have left. Maybe it would change our thoughts and deeds, positively influence our actions. We're so unaware – so unaware of the big picture."

"That must have been some session! You haven't been this animated in a long time!"

"Oh, Ruppert, it's stirred something within me. I mean, we rant like children, tantrum constantly, and don't realize the damage we do, or how short-sighted our actions are." She thrusts the recorder into his open hand. "And even if you wake up for a moment to see the truth, what do you do with it? For most, life takes over with all its minutiae that become more important because they scream the loudest."

"Wow. It really stirred you up!" Ruppert has put his cup down.

"My God, Ruppert! How we waste all we could know! And I'm no better! Yes, in moments like this, it's touched me in my soul, and then I go to the office and forget all about it, because it's pushed out of my mind and existence." She turns to look at him. "And I'm forever afraid of losing the tapes, losing the messages, because they show me there's another purpose, another goal than just the day to day, just this mere existence, with all its mistakes and hardship." She looks out the window. "And then I wonder if we create all the hardship ourselves, maybe to learn lessons? Maybe because we just don't know any better? Maybe because we're surrounded by people who suck us into that kind of environment and we react? And here's this glimpse, this look into eternity, and we keep missing it anyway." She shrugs. "Can I, can we hold onto it? It's been given to us, this precious gift, and what are we going to do with it? Should we do something? Should we safeguard it? Or does it need to be shared, need to get out there, need to reach so many others? I'm thinking it needs to get out there. I just don't know how, because I can't lose my practice, my reputation. What would we do then?"

"Whoa, hold on. You're getting ahead of yourself." He's put down the recorder and is looking at her directly. "I think it's a good idea to ask those questions, to ponder them, to consider them. Let me listen to this now, so I know what stirred your passions. I do think, as I told you before, you should share them. Start with your children. You can trust them – who are they going to tell that will have an impact on you here? The world isn't *that* small. And even if it is, they'll tell like-minded people, who will tell like-minded people, most likely. So," he shivers his head sideways, presses play, "don't worry about that now, don't worry about the repercussions – none of it has taken place yet. Ok?"

"Ok. One step at a time."

"Exactly."

CHAPTER 18

Love

July 17, 1989

Do you feel my presence? And the waves of love I want to send you? Today I am the presence of love, of tender love and remembrance of ever-lasting love.

"Love is an energy form. It is a never-ending, in itself renewing vibration form, nourished by remembrance and response, and given as a gift from one soul to another.

"Bonds of some form of love exist between all souls. Some of these attachments are intense, having been created throughout time and endlessly repeated lives together. They have grown out of beautiful remembrances of fulfillment during the learning process towards completeness, and are glimpses into the unlimited response of the infinite cosmos.

"Love, as vibration form, has its origin in the thought of the Creator. It was sent out as part of His complete soul consciousness and given to the sparks so they could become souls.

"Given free will in their own development with the responsibility to learn and gain ever greater awareness, the souls experience the vibration of love in every possible form during their learning process. To do so, they create lifeforms and surroundings for every state of awareness, filling the cosmos with lifeforms in all dimensions, lucencies and gravities. They adjust to the dimensions in which they live as their learning process takes them through as many dimensions as there are different kinds of lifeforms.

"As they progress into ever higher developed forms and gain greater lucence, they advance into dimensions that contain less and less gravity. They eventually become translucent forms that live without time as you know it, and, instead, live in infinite time and expansion of awareness, and meld into the ever-constant love vibration form of the Creator.

"They return to Him at their own free will, at their own time, after having experienced the gift of love in every possible lifeform of that created universe. They bring themselves as a gift to the Creator, knowing they have reached wholeness of complete awareness, and in fulfillment of His plan.

"Earth is only one of many stations on which to experience the vibration of love. Here, in oneness, a new life is created in a melding of two souls, minds and earthly bodies. It is that same vibration energy form that creates new stars, new galaxies. It also forms molecules, atoms, structures and lifeforms in form of cosmic creations. But it is the spark of cosmic, creative vibration at its source that sustains the universe with its thousands, millions of dimensions, according to universal law.

"That same vibration sustains the life structure of your planet. It forms molecules in the life structure of your plants and creates life in animals and humans. It does the same with the atom and molecular structures of other planets, solar systems and galaxies that are similarly developed but far behind your conscious intelligence, scientific knowledge or state of development of Earth today.

"Not too many places in the universe have planets like Earth, in the sense of containing such completely different life structures and lifeform developments and, most importantly, the conscious soul developments of love and hatred, which in previous times were called heaven and hell.

"Each consciousness has heaven and hell in itself. Using thoughts and words, it creates either state within itself and radiates it into its surrounding. These thoughts and words then travel into another dimension, where they swell into more highly developed forms, themselves creating the consciousness of heaven or hell. Other conscious forms of themselves are then projected into yet another dimension. This rebirth of the original thoughtform continues until it materializes into the next dimension of the universe.

"The universe has an overall balance of the states of heaven and hell. The vibration of love, which is the energy vibration pattern of heaven, has more radiation in its oneness and consciousness. Expanding through universal forces and law, it develops faster and more powerfully and more transparent in its translucency. The state you call hell, on the other hand, is more heavily constructed in its negative vibration forms, which rotate more slowly and retract in upon themselves on their own.

"Let's go back to fundamentals. Fundamentals are love, trust, and faith in loved ones, in souls and consciousnesses like yourself. Fundamentals also include surrounding yourself with the souls and consciousnesses with whom you decided to reincarnate during the same time frame, as chosen with your guides and teachers in Interspace. You are safe among them and will interact with them. You are also aware of your bond with them to help, love, cherish each other, knowing you are a big family of souls who have known each other for thousands, millions of years and have trusted each other in certain situations.

"You have received the vibration of love in the form of life itself, in the form of the creation of life, and in being created as a lifeform. Love is the nucleus of your entire belief of the creation of life, the belief in the Creator from whom you originated as sparks, no matter what the current belief of society. It is a belief of receiving and learning your knowledge and bringing it back to your Creator as a gift of love in return for the trust and love given to you throughout time – any time frame in the eternal universe. It is the love that exists throughout all worlds and dimensions and touches all consciousnesses, who multiply their thoughtforms into other dimensions, which become the offspring of their positive or negative thoughtforms of your current time and dimension of learning place Earth.

"Don't let disbelief or mistrust avert you from your goal. You would destroy the goal of your lifeform, and of the love vibration form of Olivia, who is the compound of your previous life learning expressions on planet Earth. You would also destroy your chance to reach me in my dimension, me, the extension of your consciousness.

"I showed you my dimension in a previous lesson through my vibration energy of love. I did this because I wanted to share it with you before your lifeform leaves the dimension and lucence of planet Earth's lower level of vibration to enter a higher vibrational level of lucence and knowledge. However, Erika is a learning process and the last vibration energy soul connection of Olivia. As such, you will reach the next vibration level with me only if Erika observes her lessons, which she can accomplish with the help of her friends whose desire to reach their goal vibrates at the same level as the love consciousness in my soul.

"Love you both, Joseph."

*   *   *

"Wow." The silence stretches in the room between them, this quiet contemplation filling the space. They've both been listening, and are letting it settle.

"So there *is* more to it than just this," says Ruppert in quiet bewilderment, and lets out a soft whistle, a rush of a breeze come into a room. "Each of us conceived in love, on this planet or elsewhere. Each of us has chosen the situations we find ourselves in, even though we don't know this . . . ," he searches for words, ". . . in our current state of mind?" He picks up a pen from the table, twirls it in his fingers, lays it back down and contemplates it there. "Interesting concept: We *chose* to do this with others, a group of souls we've known forever?" He slows again, stares at Erika. "Wow. It never occurred to me as a possibility. To learn emotions, love, hate, everything in between, in our lives, this existence here. But I guess it makes a strange sort of sense. And so, as I understand it, it's not about the hateful situation itself, or the abuse or evil, it's about *learning* and *understanding the emotion* within our soul." He's perched his lips, lets a hum escape. "To grow."

"That's how I understand it too," says Erika. "What I find most fascinating is the group of souls he says we come here with. What gives me pause is all those relationships in which one has cut the other out of their lives altogether. Is that part of the plan? Or is that the lesson that is meant to be learned here? To overcome this hurt, to keep this person in your life and work it through, or is the loss of this person the lesson itself?" She steps back, attempts again to grasp the picture. "Friends and family. So they're really our extended family from long ago, our spirit family? With whom we've made the pact to learn certain lessons to help us grow within our souls. I suppose it works both ways. That really is intense. I think of all the people who no longer talk to each other, because of anger or hurt or both, who hate one another implicitly. What have they learned? Are they in the process still, or have they given up? Or is it exactly that intensity of feeling that they're learning about by living it?"

"Yes, I wonder about that, too. It certainly puts all of it in a very differently light, if that is indeed how it works." He turns toward her again. "The idea itself is really quite beautiful: it means we're never really alone, have never been alone, and we've come together to reach a certain goal. Maybe? It's a pretty awesome concept."

"And the learning – I guess that applies to every situation? Does it? Good and bad? Across the board, you think?"

"If it's about learning, I should imagine so."

"Wait, what about the part about thoughts traveling to other dimensions and growing into material forms there --- how is that possible? Can that really be? How could that be?" She shakes her head, shimmies her hand in the air. "That makes me pretty uncomfortable. Having hatred grow into something real? I suppose it already is."

"That's a frightening thought, to think it could take on a life of its own." He lets out a heavy breath. "How far could that go? And really, what does he mean by that? The wars are certainly a physical expression of hatred . . ."

"Well, there's the balance he talked about, this equilibrium, or what should be an equilibrium so the scales don't tip to one side? If it's kept in balance, is it kept in control?"

"I don't know. There's a lot to think about, that's for sure. Maybe you could ask him to elaborate? Explain what he meant?"

CHAPTER 19

Power In Thoughts

Your thoughts, intense thoughts or wishes, be they positive or negative, create weak or strong throughtforms which in themselves live in their lifeform as energy mass in another dimension. Try to build only good thoughts and positive images using intense positive thoughts because they will work two-fold for you. They will elevate your human form to a higher spiritual soul level and will lift your mind to a better understanding with your inner self and with others.

"These thoughtforms also want to live their own life to produce their own thoughtform offspring in yet another dimension. Now count the interactions of the good, the positive thoughtforms, and the possible negative thoughts full of hate, terror, fear and anxiety. Can you see that you form a picture in your world in another dimension with your thoughts alone? You have the responsibility to form a positive picture whose vibration will reflect back to Earth to provide help, understanding and knowledge – not fear, anxiety, terror, and power. It is this ever-flowing energy and vibration which expands the universe and keeps it alive.

"You, as single soul or as whole world population, form with your thoughts your own composite picture as the astral counterpart to your world, as did generations before you. What you presently see or live is sent here. Eventually, the flow of vibration, in its cycle, returns to you. It flows back and touches generations. And, depending on how you have lived in the past, the flow is either positive, which broadens the horizon of the living human beings at that time and awakens their consciousnesses, or negative.

"You have cycles of positive and negative rhythms. It is the response to the thoughtforms of your composite positive or negative activities. This not only occurs on Earth but also in other worlds which are presently unknown to you. And although more primitive materially, they are further developed spiritually in the belief of the almighty God, and their view of the cosmos and universe.

"Other worlds exist much closer to the Creation and the goal of their blueprint. Like you, they built their own thoughtforms, positive or negative, in their own dimension, which, like your own thoughtforms, traveled to other dimensions. However, they made use of this process, and rapidly developed themselves into higher and higher dimensions. In their cycle, the energy vibration flows to support their goals.

"For some, we are teachers to guide this world in its development towards a new age of higher spirituality. Yes, Earth itself, in its own consciousness, with all of its struggles and bloodshed and barbarism, is trying to become a more advanced spiritual world. It does so with our help and the help of the positive thought lifeforms.

"As said before, thoughtforms become lifeforms in other dimensions and build offspring in form of living thoughtforms, which interact with one another. If positive, they will interact positively according to the plan of the Creator, working towards fulfillment and higher knowledge of the souls in the place they chose for their experiences, and form the universe as it was meant. There is already an abundance of such thoughtforms with knowledge in science and art, and in feelings which are unbelievable and untouchable to you now. We will show you the possibilities when you have ended your earthly life, because they are your eventual goal and will become the goal in your soul consciousness and in every consciousness of each one of your chromosomes. At least that one part can develop and will not forget the Creation.

"Think about it, Erika, and goodbye for today.

"Love you, Joseph."

* * *

The early morning light barely flickers through the sheer curtains. Outside, the mockingbird's whistle and early greeting; the mourning doves call into the space between the song. Erika reaches for the light, and transforms the dusky room into a peaceful retreat welcoming the new day.

"Ruppert, the answer came through," she calls through the open door, glances at the clock. 6:30, barely.

"What do you mean?" He appears in the doorway.

"Thoughts, our thoughts. They really do become real. And we're responsible."

He raises his eyebrow.

"We have to try to think positive thoughts," she bubbles, throwing back the cover and piling her legs over the side of the bed. “Because they take on a lifeform and become real. And bad thoughts float around as negative feelings and influence us and everyone and everything.” She picks up the recorder, hands it to him. “That’s the gist I remember. Please, you must listen to this, let’s listen together. Have you made coffee yet? ”

“Yes, it’s just running through now.”

She follows him to the kitchen, pulls out two mugs, and a short time later they huddle like firewood around the small flame created by words floating from the small black device into the room and ethers beyond.

CHAPTER 20

Achieving Greater Clarity

So, if thoughts are this powerful, what about other thought processes, such as intuition or when you sense something is going to happen. Is that a picking up on some energy around us?" Erika asks after the tape comes to a stop.

"That could very well be," says Ruppert as he rewinds the tape. He inserts a new cassette into the machine before sliding it nearer Erika across the table. "If indeed thoughts materialize at some point, I imagine they would build an energy environment around themselves and project those feelings into it and beyond.

I don't see why we couldn't pick up on it if we are sensitive enough, or able to attune to it. And it might very well shape our feelings, influence us in our thinking. We would need to produce positive energies with our thoughts to counter that, I suppose. I think the trouble is that it's easier to be negative, taking a 'woe is me' attitude. Don't we see that every day at the office, in the unhappiness in people's faces?"

She settles back. "I see what you mean. When I think of my patients, I see the small children still happy, still positive most of the time, wanting to learn and explore. As they grow older, there's a shadow that seems to creep into them. They worry over school or acceptance by peers, whatever. That shadow never seems to leave once it takes hold. In adults I see it as depression and illness. I'll see it again today." She puts down her cup, picks up the recorder. "Well, I'll ask more about that tonight. I'm curious as to what might come up."

* * *

Opening The Senses

August 1, 1989

"In your three-dimensional world, intuition opposes intellectual reality or what is also called intellectual awareness. You, as a compound of your previous experiences as Olivia, have already passed this concept, but Erika is clinging to it with her three-dimensional frame of mind. And although she knows about Einstein and senses the fourth dimension, she cannot comprehend it with her current conscious level of acknowledgment. Einstein had a glimpse of a formula which, once the time variable is removed, calculates the fourth dimension. There are hundreds, thousands of dimensions, not only four.

"There are many other developed dimensions, set up as learning places, as well as many dimensions of consciousness, awareness and development. Your dimension is just one of the lower segments.

"We travel to many of them, hoping to reach His level of constructive knowledge and acknowledgment of Him with His help. On our path, we can reach only those consciousnesses through the vibration of love and understanding with whom we shared life experiences in previous time units. For contact, we select whomever we consider mature enough to respond to our contact with trust and love, and those who rely on their intuitive knowledge and inner need to reach the next level of awareness.

"Erika, trust Olivia. Olivia is the composite of your lives and thoughtforms, which multiply in other dimensions and realities. She is taking shape in your mind to give you, three/four-dimensional Erika, a glimpse into multi-dimensional consciousness, and to show you our dimension – the same dimension in which you lived in Atlantis.

"Think back to the time in Atlantis when we were able to reach the stars and other galaxies with our minds alone. We traveled beyond the galaxies into the nucleus of the Milky Way, where Venus evolved as a comet. Caught by the vibrational gravity of your solar system, Venus remained there, which it was not meant to do. Too close to the sun, it eventually burnt out. The radiation and heat were also too great for the souls and lightest lucid living beings of mind who traveled with the comet, mistakenly thinking they could survive on it as lifeforms. They were the most highly evolved, intellectually and in spiritual acknowledgment of the universe and the highest being. Realizing they were stranded on comet-planet Venus when it was trapped in the gravity of your solar system, they took refuge on a very young planet Earth.

"It was then that we chose Earth as a learning tool for all wandering souls and spirits in the universe. It was intended to serve in the process to connect mind, soul and body. This concept very much appealed to us as purely spiritual lifeforms. We thought that here, as a unit of souls, we could further the development we had reached on our planet and return to the higher energy vibration level of our own previous dimension, which we had left to give this primitive planet a glimpse of the touch of the Creator the way we had learned it. It was to be a positive influence from a higher lifeform: We could return some of what we had learned while fulfilling our lifeform by allowing us to reach a higher dimension. It was give and take.

"Giving is receiving. In helping Atlantis evolve by sharing our knowledge with its inhabitants, we thought we had paid off our debt and were free to evolve further, closer to the Creator. We sought to be not equal with Him, but part of His picture of love and understanding in the process that continues from planet to planet, galaxies to galaxies, toward the higher development of us sparks. We are the sparks He sent out in the universal love and awareness and acknowledgment of each spark's own free will, knowing that we will return in trust and love.

"You received some of these ideas on your learning place Earth. If, while bound by Earth's consciousness level, you wish to reach a higher awareness level, maintain your contact with us. We are your brothers and sisters who have already completed your current learning process, solved your present problems, and experienced your way of thinking. We are now in the next dimension. We are the last of a group who risked everything to reach our goal, which we reached with the help of our Creator, who, with His eternal love for us, gave us the necessary trust and belief in ourselves.

"Presently, you humans are so occupied with materialism that you have lost your spiritual soul awareness to contact other, higher developed intelligent beings, of spirit only, who have been trying to warn you of impending destruction for thousands of years. You have refused to believe in them, despite their building of structures which could not have been done by the primitive humans of that time, such as the pyramids in Egypt and structures in Easter Island, which did not evolve from your own construction ability. They represent knowledge from a higher source than yourselves. They are glimpses and teachings, lessons and knowledge transmitted by us, the souls and minds who previously inhabited Atlantis, who evolved to a state of contact with other, further-developed soul-minds, beings of other galaxies, who are closer to the Creator of the universe.

"Learn to understand. Use your time. You have enough time but not as much as you think. Learn for your own good, for your soul, for your spirit and your development. Try to make your friends and loved ones understand because this is your path. It is necessary for humanity, so you can understand each other. It is necessary to prevent evil in the minds and souls of humans, of which there is already too much. The learned, taught, seen and heard negative and evil images humans scatter about constantly radiate further in themselves and as thoughtforms. Just look at the terror, the brutality and the noise. It is reflected in the expressions of the faces as expressions of the souls, and constantly intensifies. We now need every soul, every mind, every spirit of every body to fight against the destructive forces.

"You are aware of intuition, soul knowledge, soul connections, and soul-mind vibration in yourself. Never forget that knowledge within you. It is a remembrance that has survived the materialism in your world and has not succumbed to the seductions to which Adam and Eve fell prey. Remember the strength in Confucius, Buddha, Christ, Mohammed, who were all sent to planet Earth to provide knowledge and awareness according to the population's level of understanding and awareness at that time. They were meant to give the people a glimpse into the spark of the eternal origin of knowledge, which was sent with you and has to return to the almighty Consciousness. It is the source of experience, knowledge and voluntary awareness of the higher consciousness within yourself. It is as much a part of you as a being, as your sense of the universe is the reflection of the ever-almighty universe in its balance and vibration of good, love and peace.

"That is your session for today. Please think about it.

"Wait and respect that growing lifeform in your daughter. It cannot be disturbed in its growing process to become the new part of our family. Provide understanding in any way needed. Give and help in your three-dimensional world, knowing that there are thousands, millions of dimensions to reach, and knowing you will get a sense of all of them if you reach only one.

"Love you both, Joseph."

CHAPTER 21

Questions, Answers, And More Questions

Dark clouds swirl in great strides across the river. Erika watches the gloom creep towards her, a sole boat still illuminated stark white in the distance. Tendrils like fingers reach for her, and gusts shudder palm trees at the edge of the street. The first thuds claim the window, releasing tension of a boxer hitting the bag. Moments later, the entire window pane seems to shimmy as whole sheets of water stream across her vision, a silent thunder rushing to its very own secret. The creamy distortion holds her in place, and she becomes aware of the thousand little drums beating in tandem with the wind, cymballed by crescendos of light.

The ringing phone startles her. As she reaches for it, she knocks the receiver off its cradle, crushes it against her ear. Instantly, the familiar greeting, and a smile stretches her lips. "Iris! How are you doing? How's the little mama?"

"I'm fine, Ma." Her daughter's voice is restless with tense undertow, and she dives right in. "I have a question for you. Bill keeps getting these horrendous headaches – migraines, tension headaches?" A trifled moan suppressed by an exhale. "Mostly on the weekends. They last several days. He has one now."

"Sounds like cluster headaches. What's he taking for them?"

"Just over-the-counter painkillers. When he has the headaches, he takes a lot of aspirin. That's why I'm calling. Can you suggest anything? Is anything else available? I've tried massaging his neck and shoulders, cold compresses on his head, he's tried hot baths. I'm running out of ideas. We've been through some of the heavier meds, none of them with much success. And, honestly, I hate for him to take so much."

"Sounds like all the pressure is getting to him. Is there any way he can take some time off just to rest?" She listens into the phone, has registered the muted sigh.

"No, he doesn't want to. He says, if he'd let his headaches stop him from living, he'd never accomplish anything – there's that many of them. He's had them as far back as he can remember."

As Iris's voice pushes out frustration, Erika suddenly remembers a flash of a session, not too long ago. What was it again? Something about healing. "I've just had an idea. Let me look into it a little further and get back to you."

She hangs up the phone and opens the cabinet where she's stacked her recordings, and scans the handwritten titles. Her hand lingers on the tape marked 'Healing Methods.' She senses this is the one she needs, and takes it to the recorder. A moment later, hissing fills the room, interrupted by stretched garbles, unrecognizable sounds dotting distortion of her voice. She stops the tape, opens the compartment, examines it, sees no snag. Heat extends itself into her brow as she rewinds the tape and presses play again. A pulse, a nonsensical whistle, and she quickly fast forwards. Similar sounds fill the room, Darth Vader rumbling through space.

"Oh no, I've lost it. I've lost the message." Staccato movements, and her hands cover her face. "Oh no, I knew this would happen."

* * *

Alternate Healing Methods

August 5, 1989

"Hello Erika. You called me because you found your tape on different healing methods scrambled. I know it is. You should trust me even if your momentary state of consciousness does not allow you to remember the content of individual lessons.

"You received a session about psychic healing, according to the belief of Indian[4] tribes, which makes use of the healing consciousness that's present in all of us. In a previous life, soul Richard[5] taught it to you. In this life he has not yet reached the ability to scan a human body for diseases or scars of former diseases. Nor has he developed the awareness to perceive the vibration level of a sick or scarred tissue consciousness.

"Let's start from the beginning once more.

"Every atom-molecular structure has a specific consciousness. It is the composite of the many part-consciousnesses of

---

[4] Native American and other indigenous peoples

[5] Reference to her current psychiatrist

compound cells, which form the organ and body consciousness as an expression of that person's mind or soul consciousness.

"Healthy human tissue has certain electro-magnetic vibrations, which are formed by healthy cells. They vibrate at a level of about 800 Hz to maintain attunement with each other as they form organs. If cells are disturbed by acute disease or healing matter, such as scars, this vibration level is affected.

"You can learn to sense the specific vibration and energy levels of the different organs, both healthy and sick, by concentrating your soul consciousness with all its might on this vibration level. In other words, your soul and body consciousnesses can connect to scan your own body. Try this on your scar. Try to remove it by directing a new consciousness of healing into each of its crippled cells, which they will use to further revitalize themselves by building new cells with the correct vibration level, namely healthy tissue.

"On the scrambled tape we also told you that you will regain your ability to scan bodies with your mind, using our help and the knowledge within you. But first, you have to re-develop your ability to sense the energy flow of electro-magnetic forms and their different vibrational levels in the form of varying temperature. Energy that radiates warmth signals health to a certain degree, while coolness warns of sickness, disability or scarring energy waves within the tissue. Acutely inflamed or attacked tissue will therefore respond to heatwave energy.

"Observe the expressions of a disabled soul as mirrored in the mood and speech of an ill person. As you observe the movement and demeanor of that body in front of you, try to feel your own body sounds by concentrating on the different parts and organs. Compare them to the diseased organs of that ailing lifeform. Now, sense that vibration form with your mind to translate the vibration energy levels to words. Finally, let the professionally educated side of your brain understand it, and you will have received the complete soul-body picture of that body or organ or cell compound.

"The knowledge you acquired during various lifetimes gives you the skill to heal to the beat of your present knowledge and in the best interest of the ill person. Remember, it doesn't matter which kind of healing method you prefer or which is perceived by a suffering human being. As long as it works and provides relief, you will be professionally successful.

"The belief of being healed, the *knowing* of having been healed, triggers the effect of the healing consciousness and suppresses any spread of a disease. You should implant that belief in all your patients, with or without medication. Since you humans cannot live by belief alone, be it belief in yourself or God, you need to believe in the ability of the physical medication, which then triggers your belief and healing mechanisms. But realize that only your soul heals you and your body. Make no mistake: it is the energy from your soul healing that triggers the self-healing mechanisms and the self-recuperation mechanism of your body, not the medication. The medication is simply the go-between. Think about this when you administer medication, Erika. Always administer the belief and remember that the belief far outweighs any pharmaceutical substance you provide.

"Consider homeopathy and answer this: how can water heal? Homeopathy uses substances diluted to a fraction of their original potency. Diluted by a factor of six or ten times, the substance is practically only water. But it is water with healing abilities. The water cells and molecules are filled with the healing consciousness needed to trigger the cycle of healing. Reaching the cell of the body, it transmits its knowledge of healing from cell to cell until the entire body is healed. That's how a substance, diluted six, ten or one hundred times, can heal. Once administered, it triggers the belief of being well again.

"You are physically and mentally strong and healthy enough to give certain amounts of your life energy. You can use your whole body-soul consciousness to help realign the troubled cell consciousnesses and thereby remove blockages to re-establish the healthy flow of electro-magnetic vibration.

"Once this is done, you need to teach that person how to maintain proper alignment with the consciousness of his or her life structure, which includes proper nourishment of soul and physical matter. Once this is accomplished, that lifeform will become a healthy expression of its renewed path in a learning process it had forgotten while material temptations and indulgences caused it to stray.

"Did you learn something today? Try it professionally. Use it as a tool to develop your knowledge. Learn about your compound energy masses to send them into the direction of your choice the way you learned to contact our dimension with requests for help, which you will always receive from us. It is the way to follow your path and I am, in your sense, proud of you that you are continuing your learning process of intuition and trust despite your disapproving logical mind. Love you, Olivia. Joseph."

* * *

Erika's confusion and disappointment mount by the time the tape comes to a stop. "Oh, Joseph, this is not what I was looking for. I needed an answer for Bill." Columns of unmovable air stagnate walls in front of her eyes, and she can't get past them. "He doesn't believe in homeopathy; what good is this to me? How can I possibly get this across to him?" Her head shakes into shoulders that curve in on themselves. "How can I make him understand? This won't work, I see no way of getting him to accept this idea. Maybe I am making this all up. Maybe you're really only inside my head. Am I making you up? Have I gone off after all? These thoughts; I don't even recognize myself anymore." Numbness has reached her face and she sits perfectly still. "What is happening to me? I don't know who I am anymore. Please help me figure this out."

CHAPTER 22

The Source Of Life

August 23, 1989

Hello Erika.

"All consciousnesses acknowledge the source of life. That is eternal law. And, as mirror image of the Creator, each acknowledges its goal. To reach it, each soul voluntarily follows a path of learning that takes it through countless lifeforms and experiences of its choice. During this process, its path joins the path of all souls and lifeforms passing though different stages, experiences, learning processes and levels of consciousness to ultimately meld with them and thus form the universal consciousness with the Creator.

"While progressing on its path, each can draw knowledge, acknowledgment, and learning processes from the universal consciousness to experience that part and to discover which part it is of the whole.

"Today I want to explain who I am. For you, Erika, I am like a thoughtform, although I am not a thoughtform. I am invisible, but you feel my presence. You cannot touch me, but your senses perceive me, and although I am translucent, your feelings have almost materialized me. So, like a thoughtform, which is recognizable through your feelings as an expression of your soul, you recognize me with your soul but not your logic. That's why you still doubt the reality of my existence.

"I am as real in my reality as you are in yours. Your logic finds this impossible, but that logic belongs to learning place Earth. In order to acknowledge and discover other realities and realms, you have to allow your feelings and senses to take over and perceive me through them alone.

"I want to explain who Olivia is. Olivia is the compound of earthly lifeforms of which Erika is the final one, if she finishes her two incarnations in one lifeform according to plan. She is and always was my thoughtform, my ideal. I have recognized and attuned to her throughout multiple lives together, some in a lifeform similar to your present one, Erika, on planets like Earth, which were learning places of the past for both of us.

"She is also the other half of my soul; the anima to my animus. Therefore, our goal has always been to become one like we were in various learning places and stages of your soul development. One of those times was at the French Court, as I already told you. I was the poet, you were Olivia. We were on our way to become whole on planet Earth, but circumstances separated us and I passed to my current reality but you could not follow.

"That's why I have such love, understanding and longing for you. The beam I send you illuminates the path to your goal and shows you what we had together, what brought and kept us together to continue throughout eternity. It is what we talked about in Interspace to help you finish the incarnation of Erika to become the wholeness of Olivia so we can continue on our journey into my dimension together.

"Don't doubt me anymore. It will destroy our relationship now as it did before. Not trusting my love and ability to teach you a higher spiritual level, which you could not understand then either, closes the door. Only with trust in your search for the truth will you reach the next dimension. Doubt hinders your acknowledgment of the ability of souls and destroys your relationship with others.

"On learning place Earth, most humans fail to acknowledge the soul and its relationship to other souls. As a result, they are unable to leave Earth, and return again and again until they reach greater spirituality that lets them recognize their own soul as spark from the Creator and compound learning experience of that acknowledgment.

"Their voluntary journey leads them back to the Creator as the souls He originally created. They present themselves as a gift, as pure soul, who voluntarily experienced multiple pathways of experience, knowledge and acknowledgment. In the end, each soul becomes a minute mirror picture of the Creator, as the creation of life itself. This transformation occurs as the soul acknowledges its experiences as the truth of the life of that lifeform itself. For its love of Creation, it has become a part of the vibration of love and peace of the Creator of the infinite universe. Erika, keep that in mind as your goal and stop doubting yourself, your goal, or the truth, which is your goal into infinity.

"Today, I want to show you my dimension, of which I can only give you a glimpse in the current state of your being, which will momentarily let you live as a translucent lifeform with me by your side. Here, our path combines to unite us as a compound soul and transform us into one, the way we started in the mind of the Creator. We will travel as one along our path to fulfill our learning processes and return with our compound learning experiences, which we will devote to Him, the eternal Creator, acknowledged throughout all eons of time.

"Erika, that is only a glimpse of the timeless and endless dimension in which vibrations travel unified through the universe. Once we have reached that stage, we can choose any planet or star compatible with our vibration pattern to experience another realm completely new to us. This grand dimension before us contains the spectacular picture of the Creator and of us. There, our souls are like universes in themselves, ever-expanding, rejuvenating, never-forgetting and unified. We are a universe of experiences, images and vibrations, of love and peace. All this is contained within ourselves as starting point on the spiral to ever-greater, more spectacular, ever-higher reaching knowledge and beauty. We will understand that music is the sounds and vibrations of the stars. This mystery of the stars, of reincarnation and rejuvenation in itself, evolving into another galaxy, forever expanding into infinity."

"Oh my God, how is this possible?"

"You will learn, Erika, together with Olivia. You will learn to see the pictures of my world and recognize it as your future. You cannot accept them now, but you will once you reach my dimension, where lifeforms, presently unknown to mankind, exist as floating energies. It is where vibrations float as consciousness alone, as consciousness of a soul connected with other souls and other consciousnesses in the infinite time frame of the universe, which spirals higher and higher. I know you cannot perceive it now, but they exist. I know, because I received a glimpse of them and want to share this with you once you can acknowledge me in my realm.

"The beam is my love, peace, trust, passion and patience. Please accept it and the knowledge from other worlds even if it seems unbelievable to you. It will not sound unbelievable to your soul because your soul knows the truth.

"Love you forever, Olivia. Love you, Erika, in your search for the truth and we will start our next session soon. Joseph."

CHAPTER 23

New Sights

On her way home from the office, Erika reminds herself again to call Iris. The new medication for migraines would open the blood vessels and diminish the pressure Bill felt during his headaches. Imitrex. She mustn't forget to call; it's important for him. He could then discuss the details with his own doctor.

The road winds along the lazy river, and in the lingering heat of the day, this view puts her in a pensive mood, sloughing off the tension. She catches dots of light dancing across the surface of the water, takes in the quiet of the road, the azure sky as heat seeps into the car through the windshield in spite of cold blasting vents.

She opens the kitchen door, drops her stack of papers on the counter. Ruppert turns to greet her; he's already fixing lunch for the two of them.

"Great timing," he says, and quickly heaps colorful salad on two plates before taking them to the table. "You look hot. Ice water?" She sits down, and before she can reply, he hands her a glass. She gulps quickly.

"Thanks, I needed that."

He passes the utensils, and she peers at her plate. Fresh greens next to a turkey sandwich. She takes a bite.

"You look exhausted. Is this afternoon's schedule as busy?"

"I think so." A ghost of a smile graces her lips. "I think I'd like to lie down a little, maybe get some of my strength back before we head back."

"I'll wake you. Close your eyes."

*   *   *

New Sights Through Thoughts

August 24, 1989

"You called me, Erika. I will give you the strength you need. Accept my vibration of strength, love and peace in your soul.

"Today, I want to show you my viewpoint, if you want to follow me. I will help you receive the knowledge within the boundaries of your understanding.

"Come. Try to float. Float with me. Try to float and look down and see that gorgeous, wonderful planet of yours. Look at it without time and space. See it in its splendor with past, present and future as one."

She seems to glide.

"Now, look down at the breathtaking sky that is part of the picture of your planet with its imaginable, extended forms and expressions. See the expressions of ideas and valuable art lost for centuries and eons of your time, all simultaneously present while time is suspended. They all exist at the same moment in an extension of the thoughts. You're looking at it through your thoughts.

"The sight through our thoughts allows us to experience this beauty. Thoughts show us the beauty of art, music, and architecture. They let us hear the sounds, feel the vibrations of energy forms of movement in dimensions that create and enclose infinitely changing forms, figures, movements, waves, colors, sounds, thoughts, vibrations and overwhelmingly beautiful feelings. They transform feelings, light, stars, and rebuild forms. Lifeforms die and renew themselves without timeframe, in a never-ending, ever-forming process that transforms translucency with vibrations to materialize them again in a never-ending cycle of life on your planet Earth.

"Try to see it through my eyes. See the creation of a lifeform from minute cell structure to complete human being as an image of the Creator in its thoughts, sounds, smells, taste and imagination.

"Watch that lifeform grow into an ever-more translucent, higher developed thoughtform, becoming a spiritual form of energy and vibration as it spirals into a form of life that exists without material body or surrounding. It has the capability to transform itself into any translucent material as a combined soul-spirit-material vibration, knowing and ever-learning and ever-teaching simultaneously. It acknowledges all senses and feelings at the same moment.

"With the patience of knowing, experiencing and enjoying every unit of space and time, it is simultaneously a material and immaterial being, immortal, changeable, independent of time and material itself, as a living form of another dimension. Knowing that it is an ever-renewable, immortal part of that next dimension, it spirals into that next dimension as an overwhelmingly joyful thought of happiness and oneness. In peace, as an expression of the love of the almighty Creator, this vibration is one with the eternal energy vibration of the source of every living cell structure.

"Can you follow me, Erika? Feel it. Feel it within yourself. Then you will know what love is, what peace is, in single forms and single sparks of structural vibration.

"Let's continue. The most developed dimensions in the universe are the most translucent forms of the highest energy vibration levels. These levels are in terms of the vibrational level of the entity that is conscious and aware of the Creator and of His vibrational level.

"The vibrational level of the Creator is the level which contains the eternally expanding, ever-forming and creating form of love in its consciousness. This form of love vibrates into the future level of that expanding dimension, as a thoughtform of that vibrational level and so-called offspring. As such, it vibrates into the next dimension and becomes an offspring of that dimension and that level's consciousness. This occurs in oneness of the entire universal consciousness of the ever-expanding and creating consciousness of the Creator.

"Lifeforms in other dimensions are of lesser developed levels and need to reincarnate in their dimensions many times. At each level, the cycle of reincarnation ends when a particular soul has reached a certain level of awareness and knowledge in its consciousness to evolve into the next higher vibrational level of energy.

"Each soul adjusts to that higher dimension's level of vibrational energy matter, which is translucent in its form and becomes ever lighter, lucent and translucent. It forms translucency in itself, radiating the vibration of life within its realm, floating and sparkling and radiating it with such intensity that it radiates its form back as a picture of itself. It is similar to the effect of mirrors and mirror images on your planet, which reflect a picture from mirror to mirror in an endless tunnel or hallway of frameless mirrors, reflecting it as well as its images. Got it, Olivia?

"That was another glimpse into our dimension, Olivia, and I see now that the urge and love within you wants to receive the knowledge of the next dimension. I also see that you want to recognize me as part of that dimension. Therefore, our friends here, your teachers, will give you the chance tomorrow morning to come along with me. We will travel into my dimension together in a way you will understand.

"Are you awake and full of your strength again? Relaxed? Not tired anymore? See, it worked. Happy now? Now you can continue and finish your daily work to radiate strength, happiness and joy to sick souls who will approach you today. Give some of your strength to them, from healing consciousness to sick consciousness with the assurance of healing. Don't hide behind the mask of exhaustion. You have enough strength for yourself and others.

"I send you all my love and the greetings of my friends and will expect you tomorrow. Joseph."

* * *

Erika looks at her watch. *I have to hurry to be back at the office by two.* She calls into the emptiness of the house, "Ruppert?" She gets up, gathers her things and hurries out the door.

A tumultuous office greets her, and she gets hold of her nurse. "What happened?"

"Mr. Thomas came in, complaining of shortness of breath. I had him sit for a moment, thinking the heat had gotten to him. Before I knew it, it had gotten worse, he complained of chest pains. I called 911. They got here just in time and took him to the hospital right away."

"Please update me as you find out more." And then, more softly, "Would you send in the first patient?"

CHAPTER 24

Forms Of Life

September 12, 1989

Think of eternity. Think of all the possibilities eternity has to offer, which you, as soul and consciousness, can experience. They lie in dimensions you will enter after finishing your earthly life. But, with our help, you can enter my dimension before completing your lifeform on Earth, if you give me the chance, want to and are ready to. Want to try, Olivia?

“My dimension of sparkling lights, hope, substantial happiness and peace is free of physical matter, which attracts you like the gravity of Earth. Once you shed earthly matter, your consciousness is free to reach higher awareness and realms of its choice.

“Freedom of your soul and mind leads to spiritual awareness. Free yourself completely of earthly matter to free your soul and consciousness, letting it float to reach its destiny in another realm. Join us across the bridge. That’s the way you can join friends from previous lives. Afterwards, you’ll return with us.

“Are you floating without time? In space without material attachments or thoughts? Without thoughts of material behavior? Float with us.

“Now, experience the thoughtform of peace as realm in your mind, as reality of that realm. Experience equilibrium in the sense of unity with that realm and its atom molecular structure. Be a structure yourself and let yourself experience the love and peace vibrations they interact with, as well as their stratospheric sounds of peace and happiness.

“Experience the oneness within the molecular structure of realms that contain feelings of consciousness only. Feel the emerging, growing, interacting, eliminating and joining Earth energy particles which in themselves radiate and vibrate waves of high frequencies. Feel the continuous interaction of the feelings of oneness with those molecules and atoms that float freely and interact, in themselves, as the endless beginning of Creation and endless destiny into the ever-expanding creative cycle of the evolution of consciousness.

“Any lifeform, like the original structure of atoms, expects to form molecular compounds if a particular spark of consciousness triggers it. It waits for that spark, that go-ahead, to form the creative force and vibration in its consciousness. Then, the explosion of another vibration within itself triggers the formation of life in the physical structure of the atom. This life consists of consciousness with evolving material matter to form a world out of nowhere. It is formed by atoms that follow the vibrations of the plan's idea to take up a particular space at a particular moment to form a consciousness of matter.

"In turn, this consciousness grows to form molecules to cells to lifeforms, following the vibration of its creating goal. Its incredible transmitting form carries intense electro-magnetic willpower of creative non-matter that transmits a force to and of reacting wavelengths. It interacts with a different vibration frequency than I understand now, which produces the first signs of vibrations within themselves and in that lifeform.

"An atom structure of a vibration level of about 800 Hz has to stay within that level to exist. At that level, it transmits magnetic forms to sustain its consciousness of a life-creating, not destroying, atom structure to become a consciousness of a higher level or dimension.

"If a consciousness of destruction takes form within an atom-molecular compound, it fills that consciousness with its own destruction or death, and expresses sadness, fear and anxiety into the higher level. The lifeform is forced into this state of being by a higher consciousness, which causes it to work directly against the law of the cosmos. By submitting to destruction against its will, it opposes its original intentions to be a positive, life-creating form that evolves to a higher level. It also creates negative interactions within its own atom and molecular structure. What follows is a forced path towards destruction in compounded intensity: it has become a consciousness of destruction.

"This powerful will of destruction grows negatively and forms atoms and molecules ready to destroy. These create further destruction by radiating their destructive force to other atoms and molecules, which, in turn, evolve to destroy with negative force. In their confusion of submitting to the will of a higher consciousness that is aware of the impending destruction of itself and of life, they continue their divisions in the direction of destruction. It was not meant to be, but the will of this consciousness is overpowering and forces its own destruction as atom-molecular body.

"Destruction of the essence of life against its creative will and power takes place because of the evolution of that negative power. It must occur as an expression of the balance of the universe in its negative form to show other consciousnesses what is in store for them on the negative side. Thus, it forms negative lifeforms to warn other lifeforms and keep them from following that path.

"That is a factor of free will according to universal law that keeps both sides of the scale in balance. Free will exists in every atom consciousness and can be directed towards either side: destruction or life. In another dimension it was demonstrated at the highest level when Lucifer revolted against the creative[6] Creator. The image of this war reflected itself to your dimension, into its original source of atoms and molecules during their formation of life on Earth.

"Lucifer, according to your memory, was a mirror creation to the Creator. Created with the love and trust given to one's other half, it was intended to fulfill and bring about the completeness compound of the creative force in a glorious, unbelievable way.

"This creation was executed in complete trust and belief of its own awareness, knowledge, goodness and destiny, of creative expansion, of compound force for the creation. It was meant to serve as an explanation and expansion of dimensions in the universe, and did not account for any negativity or possible adversity to the goodness and wholeness of its universal being.

"But somewhere, a division of an atom inadvertently created the negative force of revolution itself. Your history saga and bible recall it as Lucifer's revolt, star wars or galaxy wars, in which unbelievable fighting of good against good takes place, of creative forces against creative forces which produced the laws of consciousness and laws of trust and love.

"The principles of the laws of creation, which cover vibration, reaction, reflection and power, initiated the grand process that created the all-encompassing laws of balance. These outline the

[6] Creative: as opposed to destructive or life-destroying

equilibrium of the universe itself and within any of its singular dimensions, covering therefore any and every single lifeform within them. This balance extends to each of the atom-molecular structures of a single lifeform and its neutron and positron patterns that form or destroy lifeforms as expression of the free will of the consciousness according to universal law.

"Think about it, Erika. Later we will follow up on this session.

"Try to avoid the destruction of your world as part of a universe that lives within the universal laws. You have been warned at various times not to follow the negative forces onto negative paths. Images were sent but misunderstood, or only partially understood, which delayed the destruction of lifeform on Earth.

"We want to help you. We are lifeforms in Interspace who were not able to avert the destruction of Atlantis. We were destroyed even though our state of consciousness was much more advanced than yours is now. However, in spite of our soul attunement, we allowed materially-oriented souls to overpower us and use destructive forces against our souls, our consciousness, our lifeform, our world and culture, our intelligence and, in the end, our creative living and thinking consciousness.

"You have already reached the beginning of our pathway. You are more materially-oriented than we were at that time, causing you not to listen to the higher conscious levels. Unless you do, you will follow the negative ways of the cosmos toward atomic destruction. In your earthly timeframe you only have about ten years to avert the disaster. And, although many consciousnesses are speaking up about the impending destruction, the materially-oriented leaders presently in power are not listening.

"We want to help you balance your conscious debt to keep your lifeform on the path of the creative forces as it was meant to be. Helping you and other worlds on the brink of destruction has become our goal in our dimension. As teachers, we try to contact anyone who will listen to us by opening channels, offering learning materials and remembrance. We also try to influence psychic channels to follow our instructions towards peace and love. In return, we bring them peace and love and enable them to come home to a higher level from learning place Earth.

"We try to influence a lifeform prior to it fulfilling its incarnation because we know that once it returns to Interspace it begins its resting state for a certain period of time to acknowledge its own learning process. At that time, it will no longer have any interest or even capability to understand the future of its previous learning place. Thus, we need you to act now while still in your current state of learning and consciousness and ability to acknowledge us.

"Erika, you received a glimpse of our teaching. Consider it, act on it and learn. And when we feel your desire to know more, we will contact you again and will start with a series of new sessions.

"For now, rest and digest what you heard. Olivia, my love, I will contact you soon. I will not close our contact; I love you too much. If you are ready for another session tomorrow morning, let me know. Talk to Erika, who seems to be tired and consumed by her profession. Convince her to allow for a creative pause in her momentary work which is necessary for both of you in your goal of oneness.

"Goodbye my love. Joseph."

* * *

Ruppert looks up as the tape clicks to a stop. "That was quite an intense session."

"Yes," she replies through far away eyes, a distance he cannot pull in. "Lifeform, expects to form, complete its plan. What does it mean that a consciousness of negativity, or evil, can take over and grow like mold on bread and overpower the original consciousness? Take over its will? My god, those repercussions! If that is really so, how frightening. How vulnerable are we?"

"I guess we have to be careful not to get caught up in all that negativity." Ruppert has slowed, a whisper slipping into knitted frown. "Well, you see it with that court case Bill and Iris are in.[7] They're caught up in this kind of slush and can't seem to get out." He nods his head into cold slipped into the room, a stagnant thought frozen across the table. He winces. "Doesn't that reflect exactly the point Joseph has made, where the negative keeps holding on, growing in power? Twisted. It seems to take on a life of its own."

"I never thought of it that way," Erika says then. A weak ray of light flickers on her chin. Her eyes trail the sparks to the surface of the water. "A negative comment, whether intended or a misunderstanding, grows into an argument, splits up families who never talk to each other again. They hold onto their hurt or anger, and it continues to live within them, taking over their existence and views in stride." She nods silently. "It festers within until it shows itself as anger within that person who wakes up angry and stays that way all day and throughout his life." She shakes her head. "I never thought about how easily that can develop. Like a tumor, really, an illness, an unchecked disease."

Ruppert's voice is gentle. "Yes. And on a grand scale, within nations, I suppose it leads to war and destruction, terror and torture. It's this mindset, this negative mindset. Once you're on the track, I suppose it's very difficult to back off. You'd have to admit you're, maybe, wrong. And when you're convinced of your own justification, how can you turn about-face? Difficult, very difficult."

She rewinds the tape, thoughts on tender tether. "Well," a sigh escapes, "he's right about me being tired. I am worn out.

---

[7] A matter that took several years to resolve

But if I don't push forward, how can I help the people who've come to me for just that? I need to be there for them."

"I understand that," he says, takes the recorder from her hands. "Maybe step back just a little?"

"I can't seem to. It's difficult. Like the patient this morning. He came in with chest pains and had another heart attack in the ambulance. They couldn't save him." She looks at him, distant pleading of dashed hope, a case snapped shut, retreats. "They tried, but he was gone by the time they reached the hospital. He left a wife and small children."

"You've had a demanding week, physically and emotionally. Why don't you call Iris? Talk about the baby that's coming? Maybe give you a lift?"

She smiled softly. "Get my mind off this? Not a bad idea, although," she shrugs into herself, "sometimes, talking with her can be a minefield." She smiles into quick shuffle tipping her head. "Will you dial for me?"

"Hello Iris, Mom wants to talk to you. Here she is."

"Hey there. Is he kicking yet?"

"Not yet, don't feel a thing. Whoa, wait a minute, *he*? It could be a girl, you know." The reprimand has slipped in swiftly.

"Sorry, didn't mean anything by it. Although I think it's a boy, just a feeling." Instantly, she checks herself, closes down tightly

"Could be a girl, too, Mom!" The sound reaches her before the flash of words. "Why do you keep doing that? You had your boy first, ok, that doesn't mean it'll happen for me. We don't yet know what it is and it doesn't matter to us anyway. Please don't presume." A voice stained with the color of an open wound and she should stop now, but needs to smooth down the pain, feels the push forward.

She softens her voice to cradle a lost child. "I can just feel it, I'm pretty sure."

“Girls are just as awesome as firstborns,” comes a vehement reply. “Anyway it makes no difference to us and we’ll find out soon enough.”

Erika opens her mouth to respond but bites down quickly, knows she’s already stopped too late, clamps her cheeks inside her teeth to slow this great torrent fueled by increasing gales of downshifting mood. Instantly she recognizes this determination to soften the disappointments of her week, just wants her daughter to agree in camaraderie and she’s instead creating an expanse of sea between them.

“Can we talk about something else?” Iris says abruptly, and she can sense the wind out of her own sails. “I don’t want to talk about the sex of the child, enough already.”

And just like that, Erika is out of words. She struggles with Joseph’s message, wonders briefly why she needed to push so hard when she’s not willing to share its source. She swallows hard. “How are you feeling?”

“I’m good, I have energy, and the morning sickness seems gone.” Erika picks up on her daughter’s stealth at cheeriness, but the life has gone out of her voice. “Ma, I’m sorry but I have to go. Let me call you back a little later.”

“Ok. Look, I’m sorry about earlier. I didn’t mean to upset you.”

“Yea, ok. Don’t worry. Bye, Ma.”

Ruppert has been watching her silently.

“I didn’t do that right.”

“She hung up?”

“Yes, I think she’s had enough of me.” Odd confines surround swiftly, keep her held within this strange circle of gloom that bruises her being.

“Well, it sounded a bit confrontational. I know what you were trying to do, but this may not have been the best time, especially the way she feels about it. You know she’s upset about this notion that the first one has to be a boy.”

His eyes seem to unlock a door, deflating her uneasily. "I know. It just slipped out. I really didn't mean anything by it; I just know because Joseph told me."

"Yea, well, until you explain about Joseph, you might want to keep this sort of information to yourself, considering her sensitivity to it."

"I did step in it, didn't I?"

He tilts his head briefly. "Well, when you call back, you can straighten it out."

"But I don't like boys better than girls. Why does she always think that?" She's crossed her arms tightly, retreating, defending and ready to attack.

Ruppert strokes her arm, and she softens at his touch. "Well, she knows you love her. You two don't always get along, but she knows you love her. Call her back later. Take the time to explain."

CHAPTER 25

True Spirituality

September 7, 1989

Good morning, Erika. It's 4 am; I know it's early. Are you ready?

"You still have not fully understood the purpose of your mission or its importance. You need to listen to the tapes on the development of the soul, its relationship to churches, the misinterpretation of religious practices, the souls' relationships to others, the search for truth and how to reach other dimensions in which most don't believe because they cannot feel or see them.

"For them, only things they can touch exist. They are unwilling to value spiritual awareness and refuse to acknowledge higher spiritual levels and realities much more beautiful and important. They cannot understand that spiritual happiness is much more important than its material counterpart. They don't acknowledge that the mind links soul and body; they don't even acknowledge having a soul. Their acknowledgment is limited to their bodies, their physical matter with its lowest vibration on the entire scale, as their sole expression of life.

"You can see that my dictations have already convinced Ruppert. Stephen, Iris or Bill don't understand or believe yet, because you haven't been completely truthful with them. You've been afraid to tell them the source of your knowledge because you're still unsure of my predictions and me. When you spoke to Iris of her future son, you got hurt when she did not unconditionally accept and trust your prediction of this child's sex, yet you did not explain yourself. Next time, give her one of the tapes. In time, she will acknowledge what you know and meant.

"An emotionally painful situation, such as this incident with your daughter, can be healed by providing healing consciousness for the pained mind. The healing consciousness needs to be given as healing force from one mind to another, specifically, from molecule to molecule, atom to atom, and neutron to neutron. From that level, it radiates as the life force of consciousness and travels back to the molecules, cells, and organs, to life itself, and the mind, as it follows the pattern of its cycle of life and consciousness. It touches the consciousness as source of healing for that mind's life energy, whether sick or discarded, and replaces that missing portion to again initiate and trigger its cycle of life within that lifeform.

"This is the level you need to reach in the healing process to teach others by using your entire allopathic knowledge, acknowledging that you will not succeed if you do otherwise.

Always remember that this is the only true way to heal. All other methods of healing are mere crutches.

"The method of Indian[8] tribes, although not taken seriously by Western society and often ridiculed, triggers those healing mechanisms within the lifeform by healing the soul, like the ancient healers, scientists and doctors did.

"As I said before, the soul consciousness contains the healing consciousness. The body, as physical extension of the soul, requires a certain amount of time to heal, which depends on the severity of the soul's disability and the time it needs to recover in its consciousness and return to the path that is recorded in its soul consciousness and passed onto the body consciousness as its biological clock. This biological clock contains the biological rhythms of a soul. Today's scientists have almost discovered the nature of the soul and body, however, they don't want to acknowledge what they cannot touch, dissect or measure, and certain things aren't measurable in material terms, even though they exist and are important.

"It is important to acknowledge that the soul is the source of life of the living being and the soul's experiences are what matters, just as soul growth is and always was the most important goal on the path of infinite life, lifeform and lifecycle. The various physical expressions are only learning processes in which the soul experiences different densities of physical matter on its way to completeness itself.

"Olivia knows all this, as do we in our dimension. You still struggle with it in your material world because you have forgotten to acknowledge and interpret the knowledge within.

"Part of this knowledge is that love is the vibration that keeps the universe together, although humans look at love merely in terms of sex, children and continuing the race.

"Although not apparent to yourselves in your current existence, each human being is itself a composite of male and female, since each consciousness has experienced both male and

---

[8] Native American and other indigenous peoples

female existences in past lives. And when created as human being, you are formed as a physical unit from your entire consciousness. In fact, your consciousness is multi-dimensional within the multiple realities of life itself. You have a variety of choices from which to form your personal reality for a particular time on your planet, which you choose according to the psychic and spiritual development plan you created as an energy form consisting of higher-tuned vibrations. Your physical existence is only part of your whole multi-dimensional conscious existence and serves as learning tool for better understanding and greater awareness of yourself within the reality of love.

"Awareness of yourself includes acknowledging that you form your own reality: the reality of yourself and your surroundings. As consciousness in physical form, you are a composite of energy that contains different stages of matter, which, together, shape your mental image for that time. Remember, you create this.

"Your ideas, which are energy sources or vibrations, are never lost but exist in other realities or realms. Sometimes they even exist in another time frame of yours and eventually return to you as vibrations. You sense them as intuition and have the chance to act on them once more, diverting them into the physical matter of your choice in form of a lifestyle pattern that fits into your existing reality.

"All matter, formed by an initial action, exists and cannot be denied. Even if actions cannot be transformed into an energy form in the three-dimensional reality, they are not lost in the universe. They become part of your identity, your soul. If you are unaware of them it is only because you focus on physical events as your only reality. In dreams you can mentally perform actions that you previously physically rejected. Each mental act can operate in a new dimension of actuality or creativity of personal knowledge if you follow through on it. Think about it.

"The knowledge reached by the mind of a compound soul is an expression of a developing lifeform. Awareness of its valuable senses causes it to carefully choose its actions. If everyone understood this, no harm, sadness, terror, envy, or pitiful loneliness would exist because everyone would realize that the wholeness of the compound mind provides understanding for each of its parts. The unique consciousness of the entire race would be understood.

"The human race is the most highly developed consciousness on Earth and should know that its physical matter consists of energy vibrations, which make up the consciousness of that matter, which itself is a lifeform. The differences between lifeforms lie in the density of their matter's content. Just compare the physical compositions of stones, water, air, plants, animals and humans. Each form of matter itself is alive and an always-changing consciousness. And you, as the most highly developed consciousness, need to be aware of your responsibility for each stone, plant or animal in the cycle of life.

"When you hurt even the smallest part or tiniest creature, you work against your own existence and break the law of existence. With that act, no matter how insignificant it may seem to you now, you hurt the multi-dimensional universe as a whole and, since you are a multi-dimensional part of it, you hurt yourself according to the law of cooperation and existence.

"By acting against the force of love, you work against the force of life, physically and psychically. Any physical form in your existence now was created to be part of your reality for your mental energy. As idea that was converted to physical matter, it becomes a part of existence of your multi-dimensional consciousness, which, as I told you before, you selected for this time and reality.

"Remember, life in any lifeform is the most positive available expression of consciousness of the almighty Consciousness on Earth. Destruction of any lifeform, in its entirety or its parts, will always release a negative destructive consciousness, which will destroy the consciousness of another lifeform. That is universal law. Creative living means preserving or creating a consciousness in its part and as a whole, which, in turn on its creative path, will form a creative consciousness itself in its cycle of life.

"As physician, you have acknowledged that in physical matter. Acknowledge this now on a psychic, spiritual and mental level. The results will speak for themselves.

"All souls do their best. Some have greater mental or physical abilities, others have less. Look around you. Just as those with greater abilities have more opportunities, they have greater responsibility, which includes caring and having understanding for the less fortunate. That is universal law.

"The less fortunate did not choose their state of being on their own. We advised them in Interspace to accept that life on Earth as it would greatly advance the state of their soul.

"Your own plan includes empathy toward others' misfortunes or inability to cope. Advise them psychologically or physically and be their example. This positive way of thought and action should always be the goal to higher realms. Got it, Erika?

"Earth provides you with valuable, enjoyable and wonderful possibilities for learning and experiences. In the sense of unity of mind, the uniquely formed plan of matter and gravity enables your soul and body to live and learn love as a lifeform from the beginning, experiencing the explosive energy of the future development to higher realms of the combined soul and mind. If you choose to maintain your planet's equilibrium as peaceful environment, it can remain a learning place for other souls in the future, which is how it was meant to be.

"That's it for today, Olivia. Always your understanding and caring helper. Love, Joseph."

* * *

I have to call Iris and tell her about Joseph. It's time. I've let it go too long. Once Iris knows, I'll tell Stephen, too. A silent sentry walking alongside her, the thoughts accompany each of her steps throughout the day. At last, late in the evening, she picks up the phone.

"Iris? I'm so glad I reached you. I need to talk to you. Do you have time?"

"I was just getting ready for bed, but now is good. What's up? Is everything ok with you?"

"I'm fine. I'm calling because wanted to explain my comment from the other day."

"You don't have to, it's ok really."

"No, no it's not. Please hear me out, please let me explain." Urgent waters rushing underneath her feet, she can feel the current even now, imploring silently. "I wanted to especially explain my comment about your baby being a boy."

"Ok, I'm here." The sound of her voice has tarnished into coppery tenderness, detached.

A quick sigh, a creeping discomfort, and she leans into her shoulders. "You don't make it easy," she murmurs into herself. "Ok. Do you remember when I told you about how the operations seemed to set off something each time? How the anesthesia didn't agree with me? And that sense of comfort I experienced shortly thereafter, those moments of peace, energy, that enveloping sense of security and safety and warmth?"

"Yes, I do," Iris says, then chuckles softly into the line. "You called it Harvey."

"Yes, Harvey. Well, turns out, Harvey is Joseph."

"What? Joseph? Did you rename him? I don't understand."

"No, I didn't, that's just it." Erika regroups her thoughts in the split second it takes to find her thread to begin, eases into the waters. "It didn't stop with just that sense, this knowing that someone or something was there and visiting me. For a moment, I thought I sensed Grandma, but, it wasn't her. Over time, over weeks, really, it became more distinct, until one afternoon, I had this urge to write, this feeling that came over me swiftly and intensely. I actually got paper and pen and wrote a two-page thing, a little illegibly, but was able to make sense out of my scribble afterwards." Reverberating hollows of a gong, and she's back in that moment of discovery.

"You wrote something? Actual writing in response to that feeling? You mean like automatic writing?"

"You know about that? Yes, it seems it was something like that."

"Cool, Ma, that's really cool." The colors have changed so quickly, Erika startles, has trouble following the transformation. "What happened? What did it say? How did it happen?" She limps to catch up to her daughter's enthusiasm, rushes to fill the gap.

"Well it was a strange sensation, picture-like thoughts came into my head, images. And their translation to words was almost mechanical, automatic-like. It flowed, I didn't have to think about it, the words just formed themselves easily. You know I still struggle sometimes with some of the English expressions." She hears the soft burst of laughter in her ear.

"That's a nice way of putting it." And suddenly she remembers the coaxing, years ago, from her daughter to attend conversational English classes. She blinks the memory away.

"Well, before I knew it, it was gone. I'd filled a couple of pages, Dad read them through with me, and I was pretty startled. Yes, I wrote it, but it didn't come from me, not really. That's what was so startling. A little freaky, really. It was odd, interesting stuff, some kind of space voyage gone awry, colorful ideas. But neither Dad nor I knew what to make of it, and I thought it might have had something to do with my vision when I came out of my second operation, but I really don't know."

"Where did it come from?"

She shrugs into the phone. "Where? That's a good question. I haven't been able to figure that one out myself yet, but here's how I can maybe best explain it: it's a kind of energy form, maybe a consciousness I can tap into or connect with? I don't know. It answers my questions and teaches me new and old concepts, explains universal ideas. Does this make sense at all?"

"Psychic? You've become psychic?" A beam in the darkness, and this possibility seems somehow ridiculous to her. *Psychic?*

Erika is unable to respond and sits in the stillness, contemplating the meaning of this word that's piped into her so abruptly, shifts her head at last. "It appears that way in a way, I suppose. Yes."

"Really? For real?" Her daughter's cadence of hopeful child-song has wiped away the barrier blocking the path before. "That sounds pretty amazing, really." Erika sits back into her chatter, perks with interest. "It happened more than once? Could I read some of that? Would you share it?"

All of sudden, it has gone silent, and she's afraid to tug it again. She breathes deeply, then, at last, nudges herself over the cliff. "Well, there's a tape about you and Bill, and," for a moment she hesitates, then takes heart, "I'd like to give it to you to listen to it if you're interested."

"Really? About us? A tape about Bill and me?" Silence spikes again in this up and down and for a moment she's tethered to uncertainty. "I'd love to." Erika breathes relief at this strong conviction, finds herself folding softly, surprised it meant so much. "I'd love that. Tell me more."

She shifts in her seat, settles in more comfortably. "Well, Dad thought it best to record anything coming through because my handwriting was so illegible. And so, that's what we've done. I have the recorder on my nightstand, and Joseph visits in the early morning hours, with sessions."

"About what?"

"Many different things. Where do I start? The soul, different religions, Atlantis, positive and negative thoughts, some healing methods, soul interactions, the reason we're here, oh, it's been numerous and quite fascinating, really. Somewhat overwhelming for me at times, especially when it's wound around the office, but pretty incredible, really."

"Wow! That sounds pretty intriguing."

“Yes. And that’s also why I thought you’d have a boy. Joseph told me. I’m sorry, but he sort of spilled the beans.” She chuckles, listens into the line, this yawn of openness, a child’s slide at the playground. “I’m sorry I blurted it out like that and didn’t explain. I wasn’t ready to, I guess. I was afraid you’d think I’ve gone off the deep end.”

“No, never,” comes quickly, and it seems fresh salve for Erika. “So that’s where this came from. Ok.” She stills for a moment, within this syllable of drawn out breath. “You know I love this kind of stuff; I find it fascinating. Ruth Montgomery and life after death and astral projection and reincarnation and you name it. I love it. It’s fascinating for me, this realm we can’t see, maybe because I’ve always sensed something more.” Her flurry is calming as it is surprising, and yes, vaguely familiar, this blanket laced within her search. “Alright, now I understand. Ok then. I can accept that.”

“You can? I’m so glad, really,” Erika whispers, sighs. “Good.”

“Hey, Mom, thank you for explaining.”

She hesitates a moment, a silent back and forth. “Iris?”

“Yes?”

“For now, could you keep this to yourself?”

“You mean not tell Bill?”

“No, you can tell him, but keep it to the two of you? Please, ask him to keep this private for now?” Tendrils of discomfort slouch in, touch silent in their urgency. “Iris, I’m just concerned about how people will feel about me when they hear something like that, I’m worried about how this comes across. It makes me very uncomfortable, uncertain. Do you understand? I trust you, of course, but still I’m uneasy. And my patients, forget that. They’d probably all leave to find someone more sane.”

“Mom, don’t worry. I won’t tell anyone. I’ll just talk with Bill and tell him how much this means to you. I understand. But don’t worry, please. We don’t know any of your patients anyway.”

Ruppert sees her hang up the phone, a smile fleets across his silence. "That went well."

"You heard?"

"Some of it. It was a good start."

"Yes, I'm glad too. And I'm glad it's done." She looks into raised eyebrows

"What about Stephen?"

"Oh please. Not now. I'll tell him later." She gets up, pushes back this rushing water at her feet nipping her thighs. "I need some time. For some reason, this has taken a lot out of me."

"Well, if you think so. But don't wait too long." He catches her mid-stride, that nudge with his eyes. "Iris might call him before you do."

She falls back onto the couch. "I didn't think of that." Sudden clouds mist overhead; and the tension might burst her head. She shakes it free. "No, she said she'd keep it to herself. Look, I need some time to think this over. This is way more than I ever wanted to say." As she speaks, she actually sees herself retreating into a shell, soft body pulled into hiding.

"Why do you have such trouble with this?"

"I just can't." The air has gone out of her. "They'll think I'm crazy. The crazy lady doctor. How will I live with that?"

"But these are your children. Surely they know you better than that." His kindness shovels into soft earth, moving and shifting the ground under her feet, and she shuts her eyes briefly.

"I need some time." She pushes away and walks into the cool darkness of the hallway towards the bedrooms, into beckoning embrace. She lies down and closes her eyes, her brain asunder inside her head. She lifts her arm across her eyes to mellow pressure she feels inside, the weight on her head a calming hug. *How can I tell him?* The tremor fills her, a murmur as clear as an aftershock, won't still. *I wish Joseph were here, real, to talk to.* The yearning inside her grows so strong and yet her hands remain empty. *A real person, my real friend to talk to, to see, to touch, to hear with real voice, not just inside my head.* She stills herself again into the softness of her pillow. *Have I been fooling myself? What if I'm making all this up? I just don't know. Would anyone understand? Is this even possible? For it to be happening to me? Of all people. How can this be? And how on earth can I tell Stephen. What will he think?*

Within the turmoil a point of stillness takes hold and she senses its presence that focuses her attention on itself. With it, her mind slows, she holds onto it, this beam of light, of steadying compass in the distance, quieting her murmur. It grows in comfort and security, enveloping her tenderly, filling her void with peace.

She reaches for the recorder, turns on the microphone.

* * *

"I know you want to meet me. You will. You'll meet me in my dimension as promised. But there's also another way.

"I know you've made up your mind and want to physically meet me in this lifetime. You will. I will incarnate as your daughter's son momentarily. How else could I have foretold you his appearance? I knew it all along. I have been building his body, my future body, to help me on my mission of love and peace in your world. You'll meet me in November. You'll look into my eyes then. Be patient.

"Right now, I must ask you not to call on me with questions. I am building the brain of my future body and must not be disturbed. I will contact you once I have completed this step.

"For now, I want you to know the vibration I will have as your grandson. Feel the vibration of the sound of the high C. Can you hear it? It is the vibration of success as only few can reach it. I will reach it in my incarnation. I have to. It is my goal, my mission. You'll see.

"Love you. Remember to be Olivia. Joseph."

*   *   *

As she sits there, holding her breath, she hears the clear sounds of the high C in her head, the crystal bell resonating within her body. *Is that even possible?* Slowly, a joy grips her beyond all comprehension, tickles her from the inside out. *You're coming? Really? You'll be here?* The smile seeps into her lips and lights up her face as the vibration fills her body with excruciating delight and love, this lightness sweeping her senses. *Thank you, oh, thank you! You're coming. I'll be able to hold you again. Oh my love!* Tears fill her eyes and she shakes them free, spilling them into her lap, smiling as she does.

She finds Ruppert in the garden. "You'll never believe it," she calls out into his restrained wrestling to subdue a broken sprinkler. He sits up.

"I've just heard from Joseph. He just visited me and asked me whether I want to meet him as adult or child . . ."

"What?" His uncertainty is excruciating; she shouldn't have come now.

"Joseph. He's coming back. He'll be Iris's son."

"Slow down. What? Joseph, Iris's son?" He has become very still and is looking up at her now.

"Yes. I was resting, well, thinking about how to tell Stephen, and I felt his peace, his calm surround me. And then, he started talking with me and I had the sense that he asked me whether I wanted to meet him as adult or child, and then he said he'd be coming into this world as Iris's son. He'll be our grandson! That's how he knew it would be a boy, because he was building the body. And he asked me not to bother him for now because he's working on his brain and he'll contact me once he's done with that. Isn't that just unbelievable?"

He's not responding the way she expected, and she keeps staring at him with that smile glued to her face. And still, he looks at her silently, and she's waiting for him to get excited about this information. And she can't understand how he can just stand there, and this doubt creeps into her and she flushes it away. She can't stop now. She must make him believe somehow. "Isn't it exciting? Our grandson, and we sort of know who he is? It's unbelievable in a way, isn't it?"

"Unbelievable, yes," he nods, drops back into silence.

"What, you don't believe this?" She finds she's bracing herself again, holding tight.

"I don't know what to think, Erika. I don't know what to think. I'm excited that you're excited, but I'm stunned, really, and I don't know what to think. I've never heard of a thing like this before and I don't know what's possible. Let me get my head around this first." Part of her crumples into his slight tremble with far-away eyes, and she squints to see him more clearly. "Don't be upset with me. I'm trying to understand."

"What's there to understand? He's the soul of our grandson. Our grandson's spirit. Our grandson! What's there to understand? It is amazing! Such an unbelievable presence, and we are so blessed. A little more than a month, and then, he'll be here." She stands there another moment, waiting for some different response. "I thought you believed this too?"

He sits back down with his sprinkler components. "Well, let's just see what happens," he says and begins to sort through them. "Let me finish this and then I'll come inside."

"Do I tell Iris?"

He looks up at her for another moment. "I wouldn't, not yet."

* * *

Erika finds herself clutching this idea of her grandson, this joyful thought caressing her spirit anytime she touches it, smiles into the quiet of her mind, this peace that's come over her. The week moves on, and, at last, it's Sunday. They decide on an Orlando outing, to brunch at the Stouffer Hotel.

The great hall sparkles in elegant display of silver serving trays cradling an astonishing bouquet of foods amidst the sweetest aromas. Sushi and salads, fish and meat dishes, colorful vegetable creations lie within glistening domains. Domed silver curls steam into the ethers, a symmetrical labyrinth of tables tinted in complementing hues, an English Garden of sorts. Desserts round the end, luscious and delicate. In the far corner, Erika spots the clown amidst delighted squeals, balloons and stories, twisting a long tube into a puppy.

"She could bring the baby here. Look, those kids are having a great time. And the food, oh my!"

He smiles with her. "I know what you're thinking, but let him get a little bigger first. She hasn't even had him yet. Just wait."

"Well, you can't plan these things early enough."

CHAPTER 26

Creating Understanding

October 22, 1989

Your destiny is to live as Olivia, fully convinced of your idea and your goal to heal, and reflecting that idea in your way of living. In your final pathway in this state, you voluntarily chose to devote your life to the preservation of life in any lifeform. In a positive sense, you wanted to teach your experience to others, whether willing or unwilling to listen or see.

"You are meant to teach that Earth was a paradise of love and peace and complete interaction of all humans. It can be that again because that's what was meant for your ancestors, Adam and Eve. Adam and Eve should have taught you not to think of yourselves as gods but to accept the journey of your human consciousness through eternity to experience love and peace, and fulfill your destiny by returning to the ever-lasting, loving, understanding and patiently waiting almighty Creator of the universe.

"Churches are human institutions to spread the belief and faith in an eternal God as perceived by higher-developed consciousnesses. However, as teaching places, churches follow Adam and Eve's mistake of superiority not only in their severe sense of teaching but also in their god-like physical appearance.

"Adam and Eve's atom-molecular consciousness is inherited in all generations. Overall, the negativity is suppressed by the power of positively-directed life-creating goodness, which is a creating consciousness in itself. But, at times, a compound negative pull unleashes the consciousness and awareness of a negatively-directed atom-molecular structure within a particular soul. Then, the cycle repeats itself in the human consciousness, no matter which positions these souls hold in your society.

"At society's lower levels, the negativity expresses itself as violence, with the final act of murder. At higher or outwardly more refined levels, the violence occurs mentally or ideologically, its final goal of murder starting with the individual carrier of an idea or ideological system and ending in the murder of worldly societies.

"The results are wars between brothers and sisters holding different material or spiritual ideologies that grow to spiritual wars of different religions, with violence and murder of spiritual thoughts in the mental dimensions of your plane leading to death and destruction of the idea. In the cycle of life, physical destruction precedes the destruction of spiritual ideals and ideologies. Only by giving up a misdirected ideology does the consciousness give up the need to fight for an initially positive idea now led astray by misperception.

"There are many ways to perceive the almighty Consciousness in universal law, since as many images exist of His reflection as there are images of souls. However, all of the images are and should be unified in the knowledge that each is only a partial knowledge received at a particular time to suit, teach and convince a specific group of people living then.

"Many parts of the Creator's ideology are related because the seed for that idea was planted in the human consciousness.

"The goal of higher spiritual thinking has always been to acknowledge and worship the one and only almighty Creator of the universe. Material thinking and the need for power in spiritual leaders on Earth has clouded the belief, knowledge and acknowledgment of the leading force within each of us that allows us to intuitively find the right path to our Creator through our numerous incarnations and experiences. We never lose sight of our goal to return to Him, at our own free will, to bring back the spark of acknowledgement and knowledge of all our experiences, thereby achieving our goal as it was meant to be.

"With that in mind, look back at the many thousands of years of development of your society and consider what you received with this session today.

"Olivia, my darling, I love you. Work with Erika to take more time to think about the previous sessions and to listen to them over and over again. Don't forget your goal. You have time, but not as much as you think. Love you, Joseph."

* * *

Erika rewinds the tape, stops mid-way, looks at Ruppert, then starts it up again. "These three weeks of silence seemed like forever. I never thought I'd miss the awfully early morning sessions so much!" The slightest twitch, a damp tremble accompanies quick exhalation. "To be honest, I've been afraid to voice any questions inside my head, I've been trying to ignore wanting to communicate with him, and I'm so glad he woke me today." For a moment, she seems an innocent child, the instant is fleeting; the door snaps shut.

"I thought he was working on his body and his brain and couldn't be disturbed?"

"Maybe he's done? I have no idea." She motions hesitatingly to the cabinet in back of the stairs, an obligation of sorts lingering. "The tapes have been collecting dust. Almost forgotten. I haven't been listening at all. He's said it now a couple of times that I should listen to them again, learn from them, but I can't find the time, can't bring myself to do it. I've recorded, we've listened, and I've put them away to keep them safe, but I can't seem to bring myself to listen again. It's like climbing a wall, this burden of threshold to step over, this heaviness, I can't seem to cross." A beast rears its head inside the expanse of her stillness, this unspeakable threat to avoid.

"Is there a reason for that?" A breath of a breeze, so simple in its deliberation, pulls at her softly.

The seconds tick and she sits still while pushing away this wanting to flee, yet mired in place. "I just don't know." A weight too great to push off. Again. She takes a breath. "And now I feel guilty over letting them just languish there. When I'm clear-headed, I feel so strongly that everyone should have a chance to listen to this, not just you and I. It seems such a waste to allow this gift to end here. My god, the insights! They should get out in the world." Her voice has dropped to a whisper, labored and warm. "When I think of the incredible feelings I get as I received this knowledge, I want to share it with the world, enlighten others. Let them hear and make up their own minds of whether this is real or even possible. Allow the information into their hearts and lift their souls." Her eyes have caught on something in the distance and hover there for a moment before resting on Ruppert again in a spark of anguished resignation.

"Well, if you feel that strongly about it, why don't you start by letting the kids listen to them? Some of the tapes are about them – give Stephen his and Iris hers. You've told them about the source, now let them hear it firsthand. If you feel this strongly about it, maybe the time has come to share this information. Start with them, see where it leads."

She sits perfectly still as a jumble of thoughts slices her head, reaching to softness underneath. She pushes forward, retreats, tries again. "Maybe you're right. Maybe this is the way it's supposed to be. Maybe I just have to do it, find the courage to do it." She lets out a sigh, this whisper crossing her lips, shadow dancing across her eyes, and then it's gone.

"Maybe it's time to let go."

CHAPTER 27

New Sights And Possibilities

Sight of the enormous circle fills Erika's eyes, and she's watching, mesmerized, knowing, somehow, that this view shows her the path of her own existence. As she follows intricate movements, she notices elaborate complexities, and yet, all of it is so singularly clear in front of her eyes, and she can see all her movements from the beginning. It is then she is certain that she is watching her journey unfold, from creation through the many experiences of her incarnations, all the way to her return to the Creator.

In the center of the circle resides a glittering Earth with all of its living things and its history, from its birth to the future and beyond. No time as she knows it plays a part here; it has been removed, non-existent somehow, and without it, she can observe everything happening at once, in one space and time: prehistoric times play out within dark ages and the renaissance, amidst modern times of wars and peace. Everything takes place simultaneously, interacting right there in her field of vision, this beautiful dance of fluid ribbons with delicate facets fitting one into the next, layers of existence playing out just for her to see.

As she keeps looking, a galaxy replaces the planet within the circle, and she can see how it started, evolved and developed, its own history of existence and events displaying without limitation of time. The universe replaces the galaxy, and she observes lifeforms, so many of them, all lifeforms from beginning of time, past, present and future all present in one place, and she can distinguish the events from one another. Stunning creatures present themselves to her now, these forms of life that ever existed, some, strange-looking creatures to her, beautiful creations, most of which are unknown to her. She sees animals she knows to be extinct, roaming in their natural beauty and existence, observes their birth and death. In awe, she watches the birth and death of stars, births of creation with lights and fury and beauty and song. She hears the bursts, listens to bangs that signal each gust of life in explosive sound, and as she hones in on them, they grow in density, multiply until the sounds of the universe enfold her completely, and she stands still to breathe in this symphony.

As she traces her path within the circle, she finds herself shrinking, contracting to become a cell of ice, cold, so very cold, within a stillness unrelenting, almost like death, conscious of nothing but coldness. Continuing along the track, she feels herself relaxing, flowing, melting as warmth spreads through her. Then she contracts again, hardening as the cell of a stone, dimly aware of life and consciousness. She has no other senses, no sight, no sound, just consciousness.

Intrigued, she moves on, feels herself part of a plant, the warmth of the sunlight passing through her being, penetrating, and she stretches toward its source. She cannot see it, but senses it there, knows it's there and reaches for it. The warmth and light bring her peace, she senses this love within; she has fulfilled her goal in her existence. And then, as she observes and experiences, Erika suddenly understands she is a part of everything.

Someone with great wisdom stands next to her and guides her through the knowledge and various learning stations, and a different understanding fills her. She *understands* how the universe works, how all life fits within it. She *understands* the laws of the universe and that, in her present state of consciousness, so much is outside her comprehension. She *understands* that everything is driven by the life force of love and peace that holds the universe together, and that without it, nothing can survive.

It is then she comprehends her purpose of life, the purpose of her life. She knows in her soul what she needs to do, what she has done and what she would do. She knows how and why she interacts with everyone around her the way she does, and she now understands how the path of her life interweaves with that of all others. And, as she does, she understands her goal now, and that of her previous and future lives.

She opens her eyes, sits up in bed, still cocooned by images so clear, as tendrils of this vision surround her, these wisps of smoke still touching her. *Is this real? Can this be? Was it Joseph who showed it to me?*

She reaches for her tape recorder to record details of what she has witnessed, sensed and understood, scanning every moment once more to recall as much as possible. When finished, she lingers moments longer, holding onto the microphone, unable to let go this sentry, surfs the path one last time to make sure nothing's missed. At last, she gets up to find Ruppert, recorder in hand.

He hears her coming down the hall, all tussled from sleep, smiles at her. "Would you like some coffee?"

"Yes, please! Oh Ruppert, I have to tell you about this dream I had just now, so vivid, so touching, so utterly stunning." She stops to accept the cup he hands her, takes a sip. "I dreamt about the force of life, my life's path in this enormous circle that led back to the beginning, and it showed me how I fit into the universe, how everything fits into the universe how time is removed . . ." Her chatter fills the space quickly, the flow transmitting her atop waves into the other world.

"Slow down, slow down," he says as he takes a step back to observe her slyly, smiles at her giddiness. "I can see how excited you are about all this, but take a breath, ok tell me more." His arm has found her shoulders, the light touch caressing her lovingly.

"I was part of ice, a flower! It was the most incredible thing. I could feel being the consciousness of a stone. Imagine! A stone. And it has consciousness, it's a living thing! Can you imagine that? Unbelievable!! I saw it all: Earth, the universe, everything there is. Creatures that are just incredible living things! And then, this understanding flowed into me and I understood how everything fits together." Rosy-cheeked, she spills her joy through eyes that sparkle intensely, random pieces of light emanating from her being. "Someone was there with me, someone who was guiding me through all this sight. I don't know who it was, he had great wisdom, and it was all explained to me by way of thoughts. It all makes so much sense! We're all connected and interconnected. I'm part of everything through the force of life that's within all of us, and a part of us is a part in and of everything else. Can you understand that? Does this make sense to you at all?" She looks into his eyes, tries to slow to gauge his reaction. He seems to be waiting, she laces her hands around the tape recorder, stabs toward the center of the crux stirring within. "We're part of everything. And when we hurt something, we're hurting ourselves as much as everyone else. It's hard to explain, and words seem so inadequate somehow, but that's how it works. It's so comprehensive it covers all of us, whether or not we are consciously aware of it. We're like one giant carpet, woven and interwoven, connected and interconnected. And each experience is another thread woven into the fabric, each life another color. And all our combined experiences, yesterday, today, tomorrow, make up the finished work, which itself is not finished until we, *every one of us,* has finished his own work. Can you sense its complexity?"

Ruppert has watched her quietly, respectfully, watches her now.

"And if you hurt just one tiny bit of it – whether plant or animal or person, whether physically or mentally, you hurt yourself and everyone else too, because we're all connected to one another, wired together, so to speak, and feel it all, are affected by it, even though we may not be conscious of it." She moves toward the window, turns to the sun reflected in the surface of the river, slivers of light raining into the distance. "Imagine: each one of us people, animals, plants, all those living everywhere, we're all part of each other. Like a set of dominoes, each stood up on end, next to each other. If one falls, it sets off a chain reaction to make all others tumble: they fall down, too. Only, instead of falling down, we, as unit of souls, need to learn to rise up spiritually. And if one rises, it pulls the rest of us up a little higher. Of course, it can work the other way, too and I think that's what's been happening with Earth and humanity as a whole. But we have to try to lift one another up, it would be so important for everyone to become aware of this."

"I've never heard you talk like this," Ruppert says, falls back a little somehow, astonished light reflected in his eyes as he slowly rolls the sounds off his lips. "I'm not sure I follow." He slows at her movement, follows her to the couch. "I'm beginning to understand the immensity of what you saw, how it affected you, this complexity you observed and how beautiful it sounds, this picture you're painting." He takes a sip of his coffee, slows again. "What will you do with all this information?"

“I don’t know. I recorded everything I remembered from the dream; I wish I could have video recorded what I saw!” A lopsided smile graces her mouth, a leaf dropped on water. “I want to tell people. I want them to understand the way I understood just now. I want them to understand what our actions and thoughts are doing to everything and everyone else. It seems so very important to me, to us, to our survival. Does this make any sense?” She turns again, a stricken breath hiccupped in her throat.

“Would you listen to the tape I have here?” She looks into the stillness of his eyes, her anchor to ground her, twists with her thoughts and fears and holds on tight. “My God! The enormity of it all! And I can’t for the life of me grasp why they would have chosen me, of all the people in the world, for all of this.”

CHAPTER 28

Death As Part Of Life

Erika looks up from her paperwork to see her nurse step into her office, a hush of distress caught in her face.

"What's wrong?"

"Mrs. Dawkins is here to see you."

"Send her right in."

She lingers at her desk. "Her husband passed away last night."

"Oh no. Ok, thanks for telling me. Send her on through."

A few moments later, the diminutive shadow of a woman slides into the seat across from Erika, wiping at her eyes and stifling another sob into her chest before lifting her face. Weary eyes fight for breath underneath heavy lids, and still she tries to be strong.

"I am so sorry for your loss," Erika says, comes around her desk and sits down next to her. She takes hold of her hand, a gesture of empathy that unleashes more tears instantly.

"I saw your husband yesterday here at the office. I treated him for the infection in his leg. I gave him instructions as to how to continue for the night. What happened?"

"He did all that, he did everything you told him," she manages to say through restrained sobs. "They say a clot traveled to his lungs and he had a heart attack. They couldn't save him, they tried everything."

"I am so very sorry for your loss, so very sorry for your pain," Erika says and squeezes her hand, quieting to give her a moment of space to grieve. "He was such a fine young man, such a beautiful person, so kind." She stays with her. "Please accept my sincere condolences. He was taken too soon," she says. "I am so very sorry for your loss."

"How does this happen? So quickly?" She cranes her neck from crumpled heap, a sign of life returning.

Erika slows to consider how to answer, decides to be as informative as possible. "Sometimes a blood clot can break loose from an infected area. If it travels into the lungs, it can cause a constriction that can impede blood circulation. That may cause a heart attack." Her own words sound harsh to her, not the comfort she intended them to be. "I am so sorry."

"He was thirty-two! We had a life ahead of us! We had so many plans. How could this happen? What am I going to do now? What will I do without him?" Eyes like polished stones glisten from shuttered expression frozen in time, an unfinished yawn broken midway. Erika takes her hand anew, offering comfort in silence a few moments longer before outlining the next steps of tormented process to begin life without her husband.

* * *

Death As Part Of Life

October 27, 1989

"On planet Earth, a lifeform needs to complete certain life experiences in the lifeform pattern of its choice during a particular time unit. No matter what age it reaches in earthly terms, once its learning experiences are fulfilled, it terminates its earthly life at its own free will and as it was meant to be.

"Especially as physician, you have to voluntarily accept the free will of that lifeform even if it hurts you emotionally or causes you to feel inadequate because you could not prevent a person's death. Please accept that you cannot interfere with a chosen and acknowledged path, no matter how hard this is for you. It is part of the balance in your lifeform. It is also a part of the laws that govern the patterns of balance across the dimensions within the universe.

"Age in years, months or weeks in your timeframe is not important in the universal law of dimensions. What matters is a soul's effort to voluntarily give and receive the gift of love, intended for another soul to accept in peace.

"The law of group incarnation allows you to balance and work out that infinite law within your blueprint throughout eternity. In their last effort, several souls, whom you know well from your previous life, reincarnated with you now to learn the eternal laws of balance that have no earthly time frame. They will terminate their life once they acknowledge the end of their learning process, having gained greater understanding of earthly and eternal laws. These experiences on Earth provide stepping stones toward knowledge, acknowledgment and attunement on the path to the next dimension in the never-ending learning process of lifeforms.

"There is a time to voluntarily give in abundance. There is also a time in which to receive without shame and to tune into the path of other souls from whom you receive love as an expression of returning what was meant to be but not fulfilled in previous incarnations on this planet. Accept and treasure positive feelings from other souls as life energy.

"Friends of yours with whom you shared several learning experiences of fulfillment, joy and peace are still in their resting stage in Interspace. They are ready to help by sending energy patterns of strength to your soul, in love and peace, to guide you towards the right path of your inner self, which is the only true path for your soul.

"All of us here will provide you with strength and understanding. You can evolve into our dimension when the time is right for you and when you, in your soul, have learned your lessons of attunement with the Creator in His eternal love and peace.

"Accept and understand the free will of other souls. Don't force your will or knowledge into other minds. Wait and be patient until they accept your knowledge, as I patiently waited for your voluntary acceptance and acknowledgement of me as your teacher and your friend.

"Love you, Joseph."

* * *

"So you see, there was nothing you could have done to prevent Kevin's death. His infection caused his death. He'd practically skewered his calf on that fence. It was an accident. It got infected. You did nothing wrong. You didn't miss anything. He came in when he came in. Looks like it was his time and not meant to be for him to live longer than he did. His spirit decided he was done," Ruppert says, translucent fibers reaching through the shadow on Erika's shoulders.

She sighs, puts down her mug hard, spilling droplets of coffee over the rim. Without a word, she gets up and retrieves a paper towel from the kitchen, wipes at the spot deliberately. "Oh my," she sighs again, the gloom rippling through her being. "His wife was so very distraught, and I had no real way of helping her. Somehow the words escaped me yesterday. I felt so terribly bad for her. I felt so inadequate." She pinches her eyes closed, shutters her head. "She never imagined a life without him."

"I know you're taking this hard. It seemed to you he was just starting out, he was so young, so vibrant. I know: it's a shock to me, too. But we have to accept the greater plan. It's not up to us, we can only influence a small part, heal a few. But we don't have all the answers, and must accept what comes."

"He's just a few years older than Stephen." She shakes her head, withdrawn into the unreachable and lingers there, hovering over untouchables for unspoken moments. "It's very difficult for me to accept. When he came into the office, I thought I had everything covered; gave him the most effective meds I know." She shakes her head. "I feel so bad for his wife, I can't imagine the loss she feels now."

"I know, I understand. But you did everything you were supposed to. You have to accept that this really was meant to be. We can't override what's written," he says through lingering haze. "I know it's affected you deeply. I think that's why Joseph addressed it in the message you got today."

"I just don't know how to do that," Erika says through darkened eyes. "I don't know how to accept this kind of inexplicable loss, especially when I want to do so much more. I truly thought I could influence the outcome. I never expected this."

Ruppert pulls her close, lets her body settle against his comforting embrace. "I know."

CHAPTER 29

Patience

November 3, 1989

Logic belongs to Earth as a necessary learning process, while the ideas and thoughts of intuition are expressions of your soul consciousness and provide the connection to us. They exist for your change of attitude, wishes, expectations, and as a beam of light to guide you.

"You need faith and trust to reach your goal and free yourself of material thinking, little by little. Doubt holds you back and limits you in terms of material success. Don't forget that ideas, unbelievable ideas, change the world. An idea needs to live on as idea, ready to be materialized at some time at your free will. Where an idea materializes is not as important as the materialization itself.

"Don't forget that your most important goal is to radiate belief and trust in the idea of love and peace as a way of life. For its own fulfillment, every lifeform needs to experience and radiate this into its environment, setting free positive vibrations, which, in turn, produce positive life energy and return it to the consciousness in an ever-lasting cycle towards fulfillment of the plan.

"In time, you will learn the patience you need to reach your goal of trust and belief. Success does not always follow in a straight line, and sometimes occurs in, to you, unexplained ways because you cannot look behind the scenes. Try to see things from the universal view. Take the time to think, meditate and connect with us, your friends who will help you. We will transmit ideas and you can choose which you want to materialize, using your free will. But don't let yourself be overcome by fear or a sense of incompleteness. We all have to learn to live with our incompleteness and wait to become whole. It is the way I am waiting for you, Olivia, so I can become whole, as you will become whole with your experience of Erika.

"Now let me talk about your two incarnations in one life, since you are curious to find out where your second life really began.

"The initial seed for this idea was planted in Interspace when you readied yourself for your last incarnation on Earth to learn patience as the compound soul Olivia. You wanted to find out whether your group can cross the barriers of time and space as humans by way of intellect and patience, which itself is a learning process and not readily supplied to a soul in human life.

"We knew your wish and let you choose yourself. Since you couldn't free yourself from your material path, you voluntarily chose your illness, which led to surgery and fulfilled your turning point and reincarnation plan of your second chance to become Olivia and reach higher realms.

"As humans, you are surrounded by so many happy and joyful temptations that you want to remain in your state of being without losing seconds, minutes or hours of your time. You want certain moments to last forever and don't want to acknowledge that every moment has its beginning and end.

"Acknowledging each moment's cycle of beginning and end, whether joyful or filled with sorrow, provides a sense of balance for your lifeform and your feelings themselves. The knowledge brings patience, which builds a bridge for the feeling experienced, which reaches the infinity of the dimensions of the universe.

"Humans find it difficult to acknowledge, understand and learn patience, especially as child or young adult. Once the need for patience is acknowledged in later life, a person often wishes to control or reverse that situation. Unable to control the speed by which a situation is resolved, the person again senses and acknowledges the passage of time. Perhaps it is in this feeling that patience is truly sensed, acknowledged and admitted by the inner self.

"Some lifeforms have the opportunity to start again. When this occurs with the knowledge of the started earthly life, it is a path to greater spiritual and mental development and another chance for that person. However, the necessary energy waves to begin the process for a second chance are buried so deeply under materialistic thinking that only a state of great turmoil and extreme disturbance contains vibrations strong enough to release them. Tranquil or peaceful vibrations cannot.

"Until recently, you were unaware of your experience. Your knowledge came in the form of an acute reincarnation picture, frightening to you, in which you saw your soul pass to Interspace and felt the desperation of failing to reach your goal. You asked to rest and mourn, considering to start later, much later, another incarnation on learning place Earth.

"In seconds of your time, we showed you your chance and what you would miss. We gave you the knowledge of returning to a strong body and environment for your soul, which gave you the strength to continue on your chosen path. We showed you that you would succeed if you accepted the overwhelming yet joyful process to learn patience this time. You also saw the opportunity to resolve other learning processes.

"You now have the chance to begin a life according to your inner soul expressions. Your previously set goal includes spiritual learning with your family, whom you know as previous friends. You will learn that patience is the only path to love and peace in your conscious state as human lifeform and that the suffering in the human body is a normal and important part of it.

"Don't fall back into the same materialistic lifestyle that has governed your lifeform for nearly fifty years on Earth.

"Remember what you saw in your consciousness: you were outside your body, looking down, choking and floating. The moment of that experience is burnt into your consciousness, and into every cell consciousness of your body that carries on the search for the truth, the only truth possible, and led to the search within you for what happened.

"It was meant to cause you to think about your reality, your soul, your spirit, the reality in which you lived, and your inner self. It led you to the path of searching for possibilities to stay, to contact us again while not knowing how to find us. Throughout all those years, the vibration of your search was lovingly guided by me, your friend Joseph. It was intended to ready you, through curiosity, to find the one who instilled in you a sense of the vibration of love.

"See, you made it. Intuitively, you learned, Erika. You found your Olivia in yourself and you stayed on Olivia's path. Would you have done it without the experience you had?

"The learning process of patience is difficult but the only way to your higher self. Satisfied now, Erika?"

*   *   *

Ruppert rewinds the tape after they've both listened to it a second time, gets a pen to label it. Erika leans back against the couch pillows, resting her gaze on the glimmering surface of the pool just outside the sliding glass doors.

"Patience is so difficult to learn," she says at last, "such a difficult thing. And I'm not necessarily speaking about waiting to buy a particular thing you've seen or the next meal you're craving. I'm talking about being patient as a way of life. That eludes me. I guess I want things too much, want to move them forward, have that incredible sense of urgency within me, and that need to conquer something, of being in charge and controlling its outcome. Letting go of that and just letting something happen on its own time is hell for me. Truly." She looks up at her husband, notices the impish crinkle in his face.

"I know it is for you," he says. "But that's the lesson, I suppose. Allowing it its own time and being at peace with it. That means true acceptance of something, and, I suppose a little faith and trust to go along with it. Once you *know* something will happen on its own, you can allow it. It's that faith in something or someone else to do the right thing. And, I suppose here it's the faith in the universal consciousness that's needed, the knowing it's got it in its capable hands. You can't control everything, Erika. You must learn to let others do their part. You must learn to step back."

She shakes her head. "I'm trying. I'll keep trying. Especially knowing this now."

"You'll do it. I know you can."

"Thanks for your faith in me. That means a lot."

CHAPTER 30

Last Message

November 4, 1989

Take your microphone, I will give you my last message.

"We have to separate again, Ophelia, until we meet in our future life.

"Right now, it looks as though Earth will be destroyed the way Atlantis was, as these current years are a repetition of the last days of Atlantis.

"Ruppert was a member of our group and my best friend, who accompanied you to Mesopotamia when I left for Egypt. I was Rah; I brought the knowledge of Atlantis to Egypt. This knowledge from the past, present and future of the universe will come to your world when the majority of the population will live in the belief of love and peace and will be ready for it.

"I will reincarnate as your daughter's son momentarily. I did not have to come back anymore, just as you will not if you fulfill your mission this time. I returned because I wanted to help you, Olivia, and to accomplish my mission of unity in this world in which I will unite families, religions, races, and the various views of life with love and peace.

"The family is the nucleus. Turning any family away from hate, envy, torment and abuse with love and peace may avert the pending destruction because the vibration of love and peace will spread and radiate further, and perhaps it will grow strong enough to save the planet. The destruction caused by your nuclear weapons would be much more devastating than our crystal power of Atlantis, and would be complete.

"That is why we have to avert the destruction, and still can, with love and peace, within the next ten years, and stop these final and perpetual wars of the so-called different races, who all belong to a single race, the human race. If we fail, that, too, will be destroyed.

"Mankind needs to understand that the divisions of races and cultural groups he has created are merely variations within the *one* human race, just as the various religions are really part of *one* religion: the worship of the one and only God, the universal almighty Consciousness.

"I hope to be the nucleus of help, because I see the urgency of the situation. Our friends also plan to reincarnate with the same mission to sow love and peace. We hope to re-direct consciousnesses towards positive thinking and action to avert the destruction of Earth and the human race as we know it now: the settlers from the dying planet who came to Atlantis and later fled it for different planets before its destruction.

"Think back to the time: you as Olivia and I as Joseph took part in the mission to lead colonists to other planets using our mindpower and scientific knowledge. Some still live there, trying to survive. Should their development be impaired the way materialistic thinking destroyed Atlantis and will destroy Earth, some of them will leave to find other worlds, using their knowledge and memories of past lives, including their belief in the vibration of love and peace, of creation and the Creator of the universe.

"After helping others reach other planets, you and I were stranded without sufficient power to leave our burning planet for other worlds. We could only reach other continents, hoping to start a new life on Earth in some small, undestroyed areas.

"If we can avert the disaster in the next ten years, we will be united again. Should we fail, we will still be united because we tried.

"Your love will bring peace, the way I will bring peace into the hearts of Bill and Iris. From there, it will radiate. Together, we will spread the idea of love and peace even though we are separated in earthly distances, but only by a few hundred miles, which is enough space for each of us to radiate the vibration of love and peace into our surroundings. Together we will find patience in our search for the truth.

"Our contact will help you remember more of the past and your past knowledge. You will help me adjust to your world again in love and peace so I can fulfill my mission, which I accepted voluntarily to be united with you, Olivia. I came to support your mission, which you accepted at my advice to speed up your reincarnation cycle so that we can be together in my dimension at the soonest possible time. We will reach wholeness as we wanted to in all those years, milleniums of your time. From my point of view I can say it because I see it.

"Goodbye, and don't forget your mission.

"I love you, Joseph."

CHAPTER 31

Doubts And Reassurance

Erika's breath catches, stays unmovable in her throat and she sits there, perfectly still, holding onto the microphone, numb to anything other than this weight in her hand. Her fingers tighten around it, this desperate push to stave off incredible sadness wanting to consume her. At last, she must breathe, must move, and the movement loosens an ancient ache, so raw she feels her soul on fire. She breathes slowly and evenly, switches off the microphone and lays it next to the recorder on the nightstand with incredible tenderness before crumpling back onto her spot in the bed. And she can feel it then, this cloud in motion, slithering into the crevices of her being, sidling next to her heart where this great empty space has opened up.

I should have done more. Did I take him for granted?

Tears burn across her lids, ossifying her being into this state of vast stillness in the expanse of her mind. She clamps her eyes shut, spilling tears onto the pillow. *I miss you, I love you, don't leave me again.* She swallows hard, clears her throat, knows she must get out of this trap enclosing her tightly, has the urge to scream but no energy left to follow through.

She must move. She inhales deeply and slight tremors of life return to her mind. *I can listen to the tapes again. I'll feel him near, and I'll learn something.* She tightens her core, swings her legs over the side of the bed, jostles the mist settling within. *I miss you so much already.* Faint remnants of thought lap at her, stroke against her crumbling scaffolding, and, all at once, she feels like a small child facing a hostile world. *I will remember my mission, I will try and move forward within it, follow your advice.* She drags herself into the kitchen to put on coffee, knows she must face this new day. *Just don't leave me alone again, please don't leave me.*

As the machine gurgles and spits, she hears Ruppert come in from outside and turns to greet him.

* * *

Not Alone

November 10, 1989

"Hello, Erika, here is Frumm.

"You called. I am the expression of peace and, of course, love. But love in the sense of peace only.

"You have sensed my presence before. I am and was a friend of Joseph's. When you and Joseph left for Atlantis for the last time, I was chosen by Joseph to come with you as your friend, your guard, to bring you peace and security.

"When you need me, I'll be here to help you again as Joseph has chosen to. I will be part of the fulfillment of your and Joseph's mission on Earth to increase the vibration of love and peace in your surroundings and in yourself.

"Joseph knows what to expect and what his mission is. Believe in him, his power, and in his abilities. In trusting, you will find peace in yourself and the intuition to do the right thing. I will support you as my friend because of my mission and my promise to Joseph which has lasted for milleniums and will last forever. For us there is no timeframe and a bond is a bond forever.

"If we break eternal laws, we are displaced from our vibration pattern and return to Earth for another opportunity to learn what we missed. I am one of the souls who has learned his lessons through experiences lasting milleniums of your time. Thus, like Joseph, I can and will return voluntarily only, for the mission in general and as a unit of the whole: the whole consciousness and as part of the idea to save the world through love and peace.

"I am the vibration of peace and strength for you and any of your friends who can sense me. Call me when you need me. Frumm.

"I think that most closely resembles the sound vibration you heard: Frumm."

* * *

Erika shuts the recorder, a lighter skip in her heart, pushes away the blankets and gets up to find Ruppert already in the kitchen.

"You look cheery," he says, scooping coffee grinds into the filter.

"They haven't left me after all," she says and settles across the counter, glinting at him with tender smile puckering her cheeks. "I got another message just now, a short one, from someone called Frumm. Someone to bring peace."

He appraises her face, and she feels him reading her demeanor. "Well, it seems to have helped," he says then, chuckles softly into himself as he turns around to pull cups from the cabinet above. "I'm glad for that. I think you need the contact, I think it's reassuring for you."

She settles into her chair, glances at the water outside. "It's more than that," she finally says. "It's a reconnect to something deep inside, an old memory, old friends. It brings with it a feeling of security and comfort, while reminding me I came to complete a task, that I have work to do and a goal to reach. I know I haven't done enough with it, and should do more." She nudges into her shoulders, her voice falls to a whisper. "I'm just so overwhelmed at the office, there's so much to do and I never seem able to catch up." Her eyes plead with him, then retreat. "It comforts me, knowing, really knowing, there's someone there watching over me, over us. It reassures me; and I know the guardian angel is really real. Like a personal coach, yelling the play from the sidelines."

Ruppert grins at her. "Well, I'm happy you're feeling better. You were at such a loss after the last message from Joseph, like you'd lost your best friend." He gets the mugs out of the cabinet, starts to pour. "I'm glad they're back."

CHAPTER 32

Mission Of Survival

November 12, 1989

Here is Frumm. Erika, you called."

"When you think back to leaving Atlantis following the upheaval, you remember the losses incurred when we, the final group, could no longer leave for the planet of our choice because we had neither sufficient crystal nor mindpower. Instead, we could only reach the remaining continent of Mesopotamia and suffered great losses along the way.

"With that ancient memory in your mind, you want to save your family from experiencing a similar upheaval in the near future. Ten years is as short a time for humans now as it was for the Atlanteans; you remember it as a matter of weeks. Time was so short that you and Joseph lost your opportunity to leave Atlantis and the possibility to stay together to help colonize another planet sufficiently distanced from the Milky Way and the solar system of which Earth was the last to survive. Although Earth has been used and greatly abused as learning place for a very long time, it is important to preserve it for lifeforms as part of the learning process of souls.

"Our mission now includes keeping planet Earth alive through the vibration of love and peace so that souls can continue to learn about the planet's gravity and vibration in form of emotions. Souls are here to feel and experience emotions to the best of their ability, while acknowledging their vibrational levels. To do so, they have attuned to bodies that have the same vibrational level and consistency as planet Earth.

"In time, your children will voluntarily learn the necessity of their own experiences and will acknowledge their and your interwoven threads of fate. As your blueprints intertwine, they will recognize the necessity of all interactions, which provide soul growth for all of you and enable you to learn, re-learn and re-process trust as one of the lost interactions in a bond that has not always been acted upon but exists. It was established milleniums ago to help you develop yourselves. As friends from Interspace, you all voluntarily reincarnated together because opportunities for future incarnations on Earth to re-establish lost, broken or forgotten bonds may not exist. We don't know whether Earth can be preserved as a learning and living place for souls.

"Man's search to find other planets and galaxies in the universe is an intuitive goal to find new planets with similar life vibration energy for survival, as we did and found. The appropriate technical transportation systems to travel to planets as learning places will be developed in the twenty-first century on Earth. With your current technology you will also develop the memory of past catastrophies and, at the appropriate moment, you will look towards other planets for the survival of the human race.

"If the destruction starts, all continents will be obliterated unless we can prevent it by way of love and peace, which is Earth's life force energy and includes understanding, strength and trust. If living beings lose that vibration within themselves, they cause it to disappear in the atom molecular structure of the planet as well, no matter what. The survival of the structure depends on the right energy form of what we call the vibration of love and peace, which keeps the atom molecular structure of human beings and of any lifeform on Earth together. It is the life energy that connects living beings to each other in any form of life. You are all united in the vibration of love and peace and if you destroy that vibration in yourself you destroy yourself and your surroundings as lifeform and cause your cell organization to disintegrate.

"Joseph has told you the story from the beginning. I can only support it from my point of view. I am composed of the same vibration material as the nucleus of lifeform, which is the soul, the life energy, the consciousness, a part of the cosmic consciousness; whatever you call it, it is the same. You know it, Erika, and you and Joseph will teach your children.

"Part of your mission is to share your knowledge of the past and future to prevent the destruction. Your future depends on keeping the past, future and present alive as your present. It is a gift for you from us. Pass it on to your loved ones as a gift in the vibration of love and peace. It will teach you the vibration of trust that you and your family have lost.

"Each of you, as souls and as part of the universal consciousness, needs to restructure the lost faith and trust vibration in yourself, with yourself, and with each other. You need to learn trust as part of the vibration of love in human experiences. You need to discover it as emotions and experience them in your souls.

"Try to explain this to your loved ones. I will send you sufficient strength and peace as my part of wholeness so you can learn to be whole again. Frumm."

CHAPTER 33

A Promise Comes To Pass

Erika has just returned to the house for lunch with Ruppert. Stepping in from the bright outside, she finds the house quiet and knows she's the first one home. She unloads her files and purse on the kitchen counter, rinses her hands at the sink, and turns to open the refrigerator in search of a meal to put together quickly.

It's there she's stopped, when a strange sense cloaks her, of her body compressed as though she is swaddled tightly. She quickly steadies herself by holding onto the refrigerator door, and this pressure intensifies again, this time at the top of her head, a sudden squeeze of a too-tight hat that starts at the crown and slowly glides down towards her ears, over her nose and cheeks, finally easing a little when it reaches her chin, holding her in place. Then, in quick succession, her shoulders shrug up in squeeze toward her ears, relax, and she feels the quick slither down her arms, against her hips, caressing her legs easily and passing her feet. It's over as quickly as it starts, and soft thumps of a thousand wingbeats tremor her skin, the remnant sensation of gruff sliding through confined space, and she's reminded of Alice down the rabbit hole.

She stands there, dazed in the bright light of her kitchen, wants to reach for the phone to find Ruppert, then looks down at her body to take stock of her limbs. All is fine, she can't find anything amiss, and already, this too-tight sensation is fading out. She takes a breath, opens the refrigerator door, pulls out yesterday's left-over chicken to cut up into a salad, along with celery and some mayonnaise and a splash of balsamic vinegar, opens the overhead cabinet and reaches for the plates, when the urge becomes great within her and she washes her hands and heads to her bedroom to retrieve the recorder, and sits down on the couch, emptying her mind.

* * *

The Arrival

November 1989

"I'm here, Erika, I'm here. I'm happy I'm here. I made it, Iris made it, it was easy, it was fast. And I'm shivering. I'm so happy I made it. I'm Joseph, I'm a boy, as I told you. I'm a boy. I'm Iris's counterpart.

“It’s cold. It’s very cold and very bright. I’m not used to that bright light. And I’m shivering but I’m happy I made it.

“It’s noisy, terribly noisy. But Iris is happy. And we are at that hospital! At Atlantic Avenue. And everybody said, it’s a boy, it’s a boy, as you knew it would be. And Iris, Mommy, is healthy, and cannot believe how fast it went.

“It’s so exciting! I’m starting to feel better, I’m adapting now. Still, it’s a completely new experience. And such a bright and noisy and cold experience. Iris is very, very happy. Mom is happy, and Dad, too. Now they will fully believe you, Erika. I made it.

“Iris and Bill will call you.”

* * *

Erika shuts the recorder, glances at the clock. Five to one in the afternoon. *Joseph born?*

When Ruppert comes at last, he’s out of breath, talks quickly. “I’m sorry, I’m so late, I got stuck at the store for the part I need to fix the door in back. I thought I’d be here quickly, but no chance there. The cashier was somehow overwhelmed with only three people ahead of me, and yet, each one seemed to take forever! I know we’ll have to hurry to be back at the office in time.”

“No, it’s ok. There’s plenty of time. The chicken salad is in the fridge, I’ll get the plates. I know this is unexpected, but Joseph has been born. The message came through a little while ago, and come to think of it, I had the strangest feeling when I first came home. I was going to call Iris just now, but haven’t had the chance.”

“Joseph’s here? She had the baby?”

“Apparently.” Erika nods her head. “Yes, I think so. And this sensation I had a little before one o’clock, I wonder if I sensed his birth. Maybe a quarter to or a little after is when I had this odd feeling of, I don't even know how to describe it, but, come to think of it, yes, my body had the sensation of traveling through the birth canal. Whoa. I just got the chills," she says and glances down at her arm, sees the goosebumps amidst hair standing on end. "Yup, must be that!" She tries to focus on Ruppert but her mind pulls her away, this magnetic hold over her senses as she lets go of the memory from before.

Ruppert points to the recorder. "A message?"

"Yes, his birth, well, just after." She picks it up, hands it to him. "It came in shortly after that sensation I had, and the urge was so strong, I ran to tape it. I wasn't sure what was happening, but I really felt it was important." She watches him sit down with it and press 'play.'

* * *

Just after four that afternoon, the phone rings.

"Hello, Mom, I have wonderful news," Bill's dark baritone fills her ear.

"She had the baby?"

"She did. A little boy. He was born this afternoon, at twelve forty-eight."

She beams a smile as incredible joy slides into her heart. "What does he look like?" A sudden longing overtakes the smile she holds into her cheeks, this yearning to be with him, hold him close to her heart. And the distance from Florida to New York is instantly unbearable.

"He's very blond. Very fair, just a little white-blond fuzz on top of his head. He weighed in just a little over eight pounds."

"That's a big boy! How was the delivery?"

"It was fine, once it started it went quickly. Iris is fine. We're still at the hospital, she's resting."

"The one on Atlantic Avenue?"

"Yes, Long Island College. Her doctors are there, and we walked over to it once the contractions started. How did you know?"

"Oh, long story," she says quickly, glides her eyes to the floor, suppressing a chuckle. "I'll tell you more later."

"It wasn't our first choice," he says almost apologetically then. "But it's the one her doctors were affiliated with, so we went there." A silence passes between them.

"Does she have a phone in her room? I'd love to call her a little later."

"Of course, hold on," he says and she can hear him rummaging.

She slides her hand over the mouthpiece. "Ruppert!" A harsh whisper to get his attention, "he's here! Joseph is here! And he was right!" A lopsided grin straddles her cheeks. "It's that hospital in Brooklyn!" She turns to the phone in her ear, reaches for pen and a scrap of paper. "Okay, got it. Thanks, Bill."

She hangs up, and dials again. "You're calling her now? Isn't she resting?" Ruppert asks softly.

"I can't help it. I have to speak to her. I'm dying to know!"

"Hello? Iris?"

"Mom! Did Bill call you? Did he tell you?"

"I spoke with him a short while ago, yes. How are you? How's the little one?"

"I'm fine, Mom, I'm really fine." Erika hears the gladness spill into her voice and fill the stillness that follows the initial gush.

"Everything went well?"

"Yes, I couldn't believe how fast it went after all that waiting! But once it started, it was over within twenty minutes. It was incredible! He's so cute!"

Erika smiles into the phone. "Have you decided on a name yet?"

"Well, we've finally agreed on Jon; it means 'gift from God' and I like that a lot. It was the only boy's name we could agree on, since I didn't want another William. We haven't yet found a middle name, and Bill doesn't have one, but I'd like Jon to."

"I want to come see you and the baby. I don't want to wait any longer. Please."

"Yes, come soon, come any time. A week or two? Whenever you can, really."

"Oh honey, ok. It may only be for a long weekend, but I'll get away." The rising sun has swallowed the wind, leaving nothing left of the storm, and washes the air so clean she can finally see into the universe of her heart.

* * *

Two weeks later, on Thursday, Erika and Ruppert ride the cab from LaGuardia Airport into Brooklyn. Along the way, they notice the graveyard along the Brooklyn-Queens Expressway, headstones reaching up high, rising on gentle slopes next to the highway, dots against the skyline of Manhattan in the distance. November's lingering palette of changing colors passes unnoticed, and the weather is unusually warm. When at last the elevator clucks to a halt on the top floor, they step across the threshold into their daughter's Brooklyn Heights apartment, greeted by little Jon gnawing atop Iris' shoulder.

"Oh, there he is! How beautiful. Don't let him catch a cold out here." Erika's protective wings stretch over this little body, and Iris gives him to her willingly.

Ruppert puts their carry-ons inside the door as Iris steps back into the room. "Mom, it's sweltering today! How could he possible catch a cold?"

Ruppert grins silently; Erika doesn't seem to hear, cooing softly to the babe, then startles. "Oh, I need to wash my hands!" A quick bustle of changing hands, smooth movements to cradle this child securely, and she disappears down the hall.

Momentarily she's back and Iris smiles sloppily at her enthusiasm as she returns him to Erika's embrace.

The child observes her in silence, large eyes gazing steadily into her own, uncovering a knowing, sliding a silent kiss of peace into her heart. She smiles at him as the world disappears into his eyes, his long lashes, his sweet curves, the blond fuzz atop his head. "Hello Joseph," she nuzzles into his ear, catches his gaze again and holds it there. Stroking tiny fingers, she hugs this small bundle that watches her attentively. "Welcome to this world, again." With as much certainty as revelation, she recognizes the depth of this moment, the rightness of just this. He would become who he planned to be, a powerful force to be reckoned with, a light moving unwaveringly in a certain direction. As she breathes him in, she can feel it even now in the peace of his little body.

"You know, Iris, he . . ." She's looked up and finds the room empty, everyone gone. "Hmm, seems your mom went to get something, I bet. And I don't know where your Opi disappeared to, either. I didn't notice any of them leaving, ha." She chuckles softly, that joy sparkling from her lips, and she takes in his essence. "How's my little guy doing? Thank you for coming. I missed you terribly." He observes her unwaveringly.

Iris bounds back into the room. "You look wonderful," Erika says truthfully. "You're glowing, but you look tired. He hasn't been sleeping?"

"Oh Mom, no." She shakes her head. "Two hours on, two hours off. I'm tired all the time."

"If you want to, go sleep now. I'll take him. He seems to be perfectly fine with me. Go, get some sleep."

"Really? Oh that would be heavenly! Absolutely wonderful. You're sure? You just got here."

"Absolutely. Go disappear. I'm fine right here."

"Ok, let me show you where I keep his bottles and diapers," she says, and her body has already let go of a tension that was invisible before.

Erika shifts the little boy onto her chest, tugging him into tender embrace that supports his neck, and he looks over her shoulder, starts to gnaw on her shirt. Big eyes take in everything, watching, looking, barely blinking. She walks with him to the atrium windows, turns so he can look down Remsen Street to Borough Hall and beyond, glimpsing people bustling across the square, traffic backed up down the street, horns blaring at lack of movement with green light. The little boy takes it in quietly, soon dozes into her shoulder, a peaceful angel resting his head.

She gently slides him into his bassinet, covers him with a light blanket, returns to the couch in the living room, picks up a magazine. Leafing through it, senses Ruppert come in, looks up into an empty room, the familiar greeting solid around her. She scrambles to find paper and pen as new thoughts flood her quickly.

CHAPTER 34

Future Outlook

December 2, 1989

Today I want to talk about your grandson as Joseph's future.

"You love Joseph from previous times, thus you have such a magnificent love in your soul for your grandson. You want to give him the world, the stars, the universe. You already want to explain to him where he comes from and where he will go: from the stars to the stars.

"But it's too early. He will not understand it at the moment, in his state. It's too early for him, for your loved one. You'll have time enough later on when his mind has developed enough to acknowledge himself. Himself, as the leader of a group of scientists, cosmonauts, on his way into his future to other stars. From your point of view.

"At that time, things will be very different – spaceships will no longer be space shuttles. He will be one of the leaders to make contact with other lifeforms. He will meet souls who were previously known to him and will bring them their past: their past culture, science and knowledge of their history, which they forgot while they wandered through the cosmos.

"In our memory, both you and Joseph brought the knowledge from our stars to planet Earth, as you will remember when you go back and listen to the tape in question. That is how you both worked together on your mission in the last stages of Atlantis prior to its destruction, when you helped transport souls into the universe to other planets. Their mission was to retain the knowledge, experience and past within themselves, intended for their future, as you and Joseph have done. You, Erika, as Olivia, Ophelia, have done it several times.

"Now it's Joseph's turn to fulfill the cycle of love in the universe. But before he can start his mission to spread love and peace throughout the world, he has to start within the family. Through his relationships with other souls, other people, whom he will contact with his mind and in his soul, soul to soul, he will give and receive the vibration of love and peace, which is the vibration that keeps learning place Earth together in its vibration and is greatly disturbed at the present time.

"The souls of Iris and Bill were partners in Atlantis at a different station in the same mission. They will understand their son and his plans and ideas when they develop in him. He will be a very strong man with plans for his future developing very early in his life and for his age. These will be his recollection of his leadership in his past reincarnations, which will be a remembrance for all of you, if you will listen to him.

"Erika, don't worry about your earthly projects. They will fall into place as projected and assured by me. Give it a little more time. Sometimes the timeframe is different in our mind than in yours. Don't be so hasty. Take time for yourself to give and receive love, peace and strength as strength. You need it.

"Have trust in me, Frumm, as you had in Joseph. You will receive strength from me in the vibration of love and peace to continue with the mission given to you and chosen by you and your friends as souls in Interspace even before we initiated the idea of the vibration of love and peace and the idea to radiate it in the special way of healing the souls, and to heal the bodies by way of the souls. This, especially, was your plan in the bond with us and others. Our bond means to help each other in understanding and trust along the path of love and peace on our path into eternity.

"Frumm."

* * *

Ruppert has come in quietly and is reading the pages as Erika fills them and puts them aside. He'd placed the grocery bags in the kitchen, only putting away what needed to be refrigerated when he saw her writing. As he picks up the pages, he numbers them quietly and dates them. Finally she hands him the last one.

"You should show this to Iris when she wakes up, share this with her so she has a better idea of who her son is."

Erika turns away from him. "I'm not ready. I'm not ready to tell her all of this yet."

"Forever why not?" He asks, then a glimmer of understanding deflates his being. "She has no idea Joseph is Jon?" He searches her face. "You didn't tell her?"

She feels herself crumpling, collapsing into a sense of fear. "No. A while ago, I suggested the name Joseph, but met such opposition and indignation, I couldn't push further. I stepped back. I didn't feel right to tell her at the time, and never found a time since then, so I never did. And she never asked, not once;

they're so absorbed in their own lives and struggles and challenges." She shrugs again, the heaviness settling. "I just don't know how to bring it up anymore." Her eyes slide off the papers. "Let's just take these back with us, you'll type them up and I'll show them to her another time."

"But you didn't explain it, that's why you were met with defiance and opposition. You didn't take her person into account, didn't treat her as the adult she is now. You didn't take her into your confidence to explain." He still holds her gaze, she finally stumbles, looks away and at the pages. He sees her retreat, knows the silence. "You know, I think you're wrong," he says then. "I'm sorry to say this to you. I know this is yours and I don't want to interfere or step over you, but I think you're wrong. She should know, there's absolutely no reason not to tell her." A frown knits at his eyes and he tries again, "She should know."

"Not now." A harsh whisper, and she's put up the wall. "I can't. I simply can't deal with any more complications."

He observes her quietly for another moment, gets up and finishes putting the groceries away, his mouth a tight line stabbing his face.

Moments later, Iris comes down the hall, a different form after sleep. "Oh, that was wonderful. I was completely gone," she says, takes in a deep breath, and Erika sees the clouds gone from her eyes. "How was he?"

"An angel," Erika smiles. "He's a good baby. I fed him, he's burped, no problems at all."

"Thank God you're both here."

CHAPTER 35

Interruptions

Before she blinks, Erika is back in Florida and the office, and weeks have passed. Her lifeline is the phone, she speaks to her daughter often, and, keeping in mind Joseph's session on not pushing so hard, seems able to mend some fences with her.

"Teething? Up all night? What have you tried already?"

"Acetaminophen, it's the only thing that's worked. The gel to numb his gums seems to have no effect, and I hate to see him in such pain. He needs something to quiet the pain from the inside, I believe. Any suggestions? I hate to put him on constant meds. He's too young. I don't want to, but when the pain comes in waves for two to three days, I give it to him every four hours."

"I don't like that either, I agree with you. Wait, Ruppert just walked in, let me ask him about it."

"I heard you," Ruppert says and takes the phone. "Iris, check the health food store for homeopathic little pills. See if they have Chamomile and Calcium Phosphate. Just one or two of the little pills that have the strength of 6X ought to help. Especially after you've given it to him a few times. It will prompt his own healing to take over. They'll melt on his tongue right away, no worry about him choking. Ok? Call me tomorrow or the day after. Let me know how it turns out."

"Thanks Dad. I'll try that. I love you both."

"Love you too; let me know."

* * *

Barriers

January 4, 1990

"Erika, here is Frumm.

"I cannot overcome the barrier between us. I can only break through it once in a while, which is when you feel me as strength, as the vibration of strength and tender loving care. I want to give you so much more of my vibrations of peace, strength and love, especially now when you need me most. But I cannot get past the mental barrier you built. Please open up and relax. Meditate and try to reach the outer space vibrations to expand your horizon, expand your mental ability to receive vibrational waves outside your three-dimensional existence.

"We are many here who want to help you with your goals. I promised you I would continue the help that Joseph started, but it is very difficult for me to break through your resistance. Without the help of my friends, your previous friends, I would not have been able to do it now.

"Please give me and us your help in terms of trust and love because it is this beam on which our mutual energy pattern can travel together to fulfill the promise we made to each other: to be there in the hour of need no matter what happens.

"But barriers built by impatience, emotional upset and frustration, as well as the distrust from your side block our contact and will continue to do so.

"Don't you know you will be what you think you will be? You will grow in material ways according to your mental blueprint. If you give up your mental blueprint as direction, how can your material substance particles grow in the right direction and weave the necessary connections along the necessary paths within your time unit to materialize your woven blueprint?

"You don't have too much time left. Try to connect the lost threads in the blueprint carpet of your future, literally speaking. We will help you as long as you sense my vibration, as long as you feel the strength pouring onto you. You can be sure we are around you even if we are not reacting as you expected. We have another view of the situation, but nevertheless the outcome will be the same: you will see a positive, miraculous path into your and your family's future. Our future, too.

"We see you are trying to apply alternative medicine with success – see how nicely Joseph reacted to homeopathy. As will others, if you try.

"Try to understand to receive the vibration of love and peace wherever it shows up and in whatever vibration it affects you. As long as you feel its presence, it will heal, not only you, but also your surroundings. Remember, the vibration of love and peace is the substance, the glue to keep the particles of your body together, as it is the glue that keeps you in your lifeform.

"See, today you were open to your lecture.

"Frumm."

*   *   *

Erika sits within her silence, aware of fleeting energy within her, dissipating like mist in the morning sun. She senses a void, this distraction in the distance, cobbled with a certain defiance. *What is the matter with me?* And it occurs to her then that she is sad over Joseph's absence, his distance from her life as he grows up so very far away from her, and part of her is angry at the void he has left by becoming her grandson. And she cannot make the time she would like to see him, because they need her here, they all need her here and she cannot get away. It eats away at her, quietly on the inside; she can see it now that she's upset.

"Oh, Ruppert, I don't know. I find myself closing the door, I don't even want to go there anymore. I don't want to open up anymore, I'm so sad to have lost my connection with Joseph. Now I find it just takes so much energy and I don't seem to have it with all the patients, and I worry about Iris and Bill, and the rest of our lives. I also worry about my own health, and where it will lead and oh, I just don't know. This message from Frumm is right, I'm afraid, I can feel their presence push me, and on some levels I resent it, but I know they're just trying. Something's deflated inside me, I miss Joseph and our connection, and it's just so very different now." Her words sway between confusion and exhaustion, the exhilaration from just weeks ago gone out of her.

He contemplates her quietly from beneath hooded eyes circling her intently. "Well, it depends on what you want, really. I know how busy you are at the office, but do you really have to be? Can't you ask them to schedule the load just little lighter? Or let's see if we can find someone else to help us? Maybe Stephen could join; have you spoken to him about that? We need to do something differently; I see how worn out you are." A salute to colors, simple recognition of what is, and he's said it plainly, still its impact is raw. He tries again. "I think that's part of your distress: you are exhausted and don't have the energy for yet another thing, even if those sessions and messages bring you a certain peace. Is that it? And of course you miss Joseph. I can understand that completely. The connection you two had is very special. It's clearly quite different than the one to Frumm, but then, you don't know enough about Frumm, perhaps? Or maybe your disappointment is taking over your perception?"

"I just have my limits; I find myself pushed to the outer edges," she says, a soft moan escaping her lips as she turns away from him, cradling the view of the water in the distance. "I've sensed them around me, but I've ignored them. I know I've done my part to keep them away. It's just another responsibility that I can't take on anymore, don't want to, can't rally the strength. Joseph came almost daily, his presence helped me even when he didn't say anything, but I guess I'm resisting Frumm's energy, this friend who, I suppose, is also my friend. I don't know, maybe I'm simply mourning the loss of my sessions with Joseph."

"Well, I think you should cut yourself some slack. Don't be so hard on yourself. Take a break, even a short one. You're pretty tough with yourself and I don't think that's necessary. Maybe you could share some of these tasks with your loved ones. You know, maybe it's time you share these messages with Iris. Start there. Maybe she can help you continue, open up. Give her some credit. Give her the one about her and Bill. Start with that."

His words caress the barrier she's erected so silently, nudging her into a place that softens the most vulnerable edges at last. She breathes into her pain and exhales slowly. "Ok, I'm beginning to see it, I just got the word 'mistrust' in my head, and I know I have to overcome that. Ok, maybe I do need to trust her more, trust her with this, maybe I need to?" A ramble, quick flood to smooth the stones, and she finds her anchor in steady eyes, as Ruppert locks her gaze into the space she needs.

"Ok. I'll dig out the tape so you can send it to her. I'll do that this afternoon," he says and turns to her.

"Ok," she falters. "I promise."

*　　*　　*

Jon is eight months old. Erika has counted the time in her head, feels the passage of hours in the ache of her body sidled against joy.

It's afternoon when she picks up the phone to excitement in Iris's greeting. "I just listened to the tapes. They're fantastic! It's unbelievable. Why didn't you tell me about this before? Wow, what an incredible being, this Joseph. And those messages? I'm floored."

She's silenced in her confusion, this doubt lifting and layering between the spheres, and still she can't let go of some resentment. "Well, I tried." She catches the snag in her voice, redirects her singsong into truth. "I was doubtful, afraid, really. You know, when I reacted so severely to the anesthesia, and the nurses looked at me with such disdain, I just couldn't risk exposing yet another strangeness to anyone. I just couldn't do it. Seeing your reaction now, so positive, I'm sorry I let it go so long. I guess I wasn't able to trust anyone, was afraid to trust myself with this mystery, and, really, I was afraid of your reaction."

"Oh no! I'm sorry about that. And I'm sorry I've been snippy and short with you and argumentative, I know I've been too blunt and upset. I guess I've been stressed out, too. But this is fantastic! What a gift! It's incredible. I didn't really understand when you mentioned it to me so long ago, I didn't get it. I thought I had, but I see now that I hadn't." The melody of her voice has crept in a quiet exhilaration, she notices, ever so softly, this possibility of reconnecting on another plane. Erika listens into the chatter that continues into her ear. "I don't know if I was unable to listen or in another world, or you really weren't able to express yourself in a way I could understand. But that doesn't matter now, does it? Thank you so much for sending these to me now. And trusting me with them. Have these sessions continued? Do you still get them now?"

Questions like waterfalls, and Erika still can't quite follow, can't quite grasp the ribbon to comprehend. What was this turn of situation? Had she worried needlessly? She takes a breath in the silence. "Well, I used to get a lot of them, and on pretty much a regular basis. But now, I seem unable to perceive much, I'm blocked somehow, it's like I've lost my connection, my thread to this other existence."

"But why? Why would you stop? What would make it stop?"

"I don't know, I'm pre-occupied, I think. And it's different now. Joseph and I had something very special; I just don't quite feel it anymore now. I don't know, maybe I'm just making this up," For a moment, Erika is lost in sorrow, so near the surface. *I miss you, Joseph.* "Well, sometimes they make their way through my exhaustion. There's a lot going on at the office."

"That's too bad," Iris counters, and she can hear the disappointment in her voice, hovering in the stillness.

Erika remains quiet. At last she says, "I do pick up on the feeling that they're around, and that gives me a certain strength, but I just don't seem to have it in me anymore for sessions or more intense contact. I'd have to open up more, I suppose, allow it. Maybe I don't, maybe I'm too shut down. I still sense them around me, though."

"What will you do with all this?"

"What do you mean?"

"I mean, you can't just sit on this. This is fantastic. It feels to me that others should get a chance to listen to some of these concepts. Say, would you be willing to let me listen to some of the other messages? It doesn't have to be any of the personal ones, if there are any, by any means. But if there's something else you think I might be interested in, I'd love to hear."

"Really?"

"Oh absolutely. I'd listen to all of them."

"All of them? Well let me think about it. There were a lot of subjects, a lot of areas of thought, and, you're right, some are very private, but, sure, I could lend you some of the others and introduce you to the subjects Joseph discussed."

"Like what?"

"Well, there's Atlantis and religions and how we all came to be, and our purpose, really, and reincarnation."

"He talked about all of that? Wow. Well, I'd really be interested. And I'd keep the tapes safe and return them to you, of course."

"Ok then. I don't want to send them because I don't want to take a chance of losing them, but next time I come, I'll bring some, I promise. And if you're here, you could listen to them here, of course, too."

"Hey, and I could transcribe them, if you'd like. I'm home anyway with the baby, and have some time while he's sleeping. That way, maybe they're better accessible to you."

A rush of the wind grazes Erika, startling her. "I hadn't thought about that."

"Well think about it. If it's such a wealth of information as you describe, maybe you could do something with them, get them out there. When did all this start?"

"A good year before you got pregnant. Like I told you, a little after my operation and first regression."

"That sounds so fascinating! Regression. It's like you've entered an untouchable realm of life that I find so interesting. I've always wondered about what else is out there." She slows for a minute, swirling excitement frightening Erika somehow, these tendrils gluing at her and pulling her into the unknown. "Have you thought about putting it into a book? Sharing it with others that way?"

"A book? God no! Who'd read that. Fantasies of the crazy German lady doctor? Iris, really!"

"Oh my god, no, don't take it that way. That's not it! I don't think these are fantasies at all, I doubt anyone else would either. It's fantastic. I think people would want to know what's out there, what might be in store, and I think it would help some to realize they're not alone, there are helpers to guide us along the way, even if we don't feel or sense them, or want them for that matter! And there's stuff we can't see or measure or otherwise comprehend. I think there'd be an interest."

"Oh, honey, what would my patients think? I might as well close up shop now."

"Ma, really! I think you're thinking too much into it. Anyway, think about it. If it's meant to be, maybe it'll happen."

"It's just more than I can take right now. Please just leave it be. I know you're excited about this, but please, give me some time to think."

"Sure Ma, I'm sorry if I've overrun you in any way. It's just that it *is* really something."

"I'll call you back with this." The urge to get off the phone has become overbearing, and Erika finds it hard to breathe. A tug at her chest, her hand presses against her heart to still its beating. "I'll look through the tapes and will pick out one or two for you to start with."

"Thank you! Awesome. I can't wait. I'll talk to you tomorrow."

Erika hangs up the phone, stunned into place by a thousand thoughts raining down on her. *What do I do? What do I do? I've opened the door and can't shut it anymore. What if people were to find out my identity? That it's me behind those tapes? Will I lose my reputation? My patients? Could this ruin it all?*

She pushes away the phone, comes into the living room where Ruppert is reading, stands in front of him, a picture of wavering warrior, uncertain but ready to fight.

"I'm not so sure this was a good idea." Her eyes lay blame, she knows it but can't seem to pull it back.

"What?"

"To tell Iris. She's talking about a book, good god!" Jerky movement betrays her fright even to herself. She clamps down on her hands. "I can't even go there. I can't let anyone know. How can I let anyone know?"

“Just breathe. Relax. It’s not the end of the world, it’s not a bad thing.” He looks at her squarely. “Listen to me, first of all, no one has to know it’s you. Second, the information is phenomenal, it is a fascinating history and story of love and wisdom and hope, of bonds that last forever, beyond lifetimes. It’s a beautiful story, just think about all the people who have no hope, who might glimmer hope with Joseph’s messages. That we’re all connected? That we’re not alone? Who wouldn’t want to know that? Give Iris a chance. Let her listen to the tapes. Allow her this access. I think it would be alright.” He steps back just a little then, giving her space. “Anyway, keep the tapes with the personal information. That has no place there anyway.”

She has moved to the window and the glimmering water beyond, the expanse of the wide river to the strip of dark on the other side, the silence of its current, the brilliant jots of sunshine blurring the surface. “Alright,” she says at last as she turns to face him. “Alright, I’ll do it. I’ll look through the tapes.” She moves expectantly, a part of her slumping slightly under the weight. “Would you help me with that? Find ones to give her?”

“Of course I’ll help you. We can do it now, if you want.”

She takes his arm, he pulls her into him and they stand there together for a long time.

CHAPTER 36

Leap Of Faith

Walking into the house, Erika adds the papers in her arms to the stack growing sharply on the crescent top of the small table hugging the wall. "I have to somehow get through this paperwork by the end of this month. I don't know how I'll manage. There don't seem to be enough hours in the day."

Ruppert side-steps her and into the kitchen. "I know, sometimes I think these extras take our last reserves. But they, too, need to get done." He opens the refrigerator door, scans the shelves. "Want something to drink?"

"Please," she says. "Something cold, anything."

The ice-maker crunches cubes into the glass. "Hungry? Cook or go out?"

"I can't move; I'm too worn out today," she calls from the couch, waits for him.

"Yes, today seemed especially difficult. What did Iris say when she called; is everything alright?" He says as he hands her the glass of ice water. She takes it gratefully from his hands.

"She says she spends most of her time at the playground, where he's hands-on in the sandbox," she says. "I can picture it. Anyway, he's making friends quickly, loves the swing, but the sandbox more, and climbing up and down stoops on their way to anywhere." She chuckles into the image of the small, strong-willed blond boy hugging the fat banisters in brownstone Brooklyn, stepping, stepping up and up on legs the size of the steps themselves. "I think she's given up trying to get anywhere on time – it must take her forever to maneuver through the streets." She takes a sip. "She says she can never take her eyes off him, and, yes, I can see that! She promised to send more pictures." A flurry of answers, a push from within, and she takes a breath. "And she's also asked me about the tapes again."

Ruppert sits down next to her. "That's good, isn't it? Sounds like he's a handful."

"He does! But the tapes, I just don't know."

"You're getting cold feet again? Really?" His eyes knit together. "Don't. Don't retreat. You'll do fine. It'll be fine. Trust her."

"I'm ambivalent, just back and forth on this. I'm afraid to let them out of my hands. I'm afraid someone will find out it's me behind it and will ruin everything I worked for." All at once the idea has become daunting.

"Don't," he says before her mind can scramble further down the path. "Don't be," he says again. "I know you're very private and this idea is so very foreign to you, but trust her. She's got a good head on her shoulders. Tell her your concerns, your fears. Let her understand you. She will. She'll abide by your wishes. You know that." He gets up to go into the kitchen. "I'm going to stir-fry some veggies. And I think we have some shrimp in the freezer. Are you up for that?"

"That'd be great, actually." She slumps into the cushions, beneath the whip of thoughts crashing into her, hunting her down.

"And, Erika? Iris is curious. I'm sure she's curious as to who this son of hers really is. There's no harm in letting her know."

Silence stretches in the room, an uncomfortable waiting for a response, a weighing of options. "I suppose you're right," she finally says. "Ok, ok. I feel snowed under, that's all, especially with all the work that's piled up over there." Her eyes roll to the edges of the documents huddled against the wall. "And I don't really sense them around me anymore, any of them." Her voice slinks off, a sadness to its edges. "I suppose it's over anyway."

* * *

Reassurance

August 3, 1991

"Erika, here is Frumm.

"You are so involved in your three-dimensional life that it is difficult to help you with the necessary advancement of your soul.

"As for any lifeform, your only and infinite goal as human being is to continue on your written path into your future to achieve purity, and to find, and transmit to others the vibration of love and peace, thereby working against the destructive forces that are currently overwhelmingly in force. That is your plan, as part of a race fulfilling its blueprint.

"Look for the truth, the only truth, physically, mentally and spiritually, and you will sense how to accomplish your mission. But don't be greedy. Don't want to have it all your way. There are different views to each situation that build the puzzle of the big picture. Always keep the big picture in mind as your eternal goal and don't be frustrated if things don't meet your own expectations. You can always use your free will when deciding which direction to follow. Remember, life in your lifeform is a chain of learning experiences and not always a smooth ride.

"You have again reached an important window where we can help if and when you ask for it, like today. If you are silent, we are silent. We don't want to intrude. We can only suggest. We don't want to direct or suppress your free will in the decisions of your present life, but my hands are tied if you don't listen to us. Please accept that.

"Vibration, commitment, direction and communication are our ways to influence sensitive souls who can accept our commitment and feel our vibration. Therefore please stay tuned in and receptive and I will guide you in the right direction using my point of view.

"I know you are trying to weave the threads together but some paths won't let themselves be woven into a pattern at the moment. Don't worry about it. The pattern will emerge in a little while. Believe in it, believe in me.

"Cooperate with Iris's search. Let her listen to all the tapes and then she will connect with me as she wants to and as she thinks she has a right to. And she is right.

"I promise that many things will happen as Jon grows older. Soon, an inner urge will grow in him to find out more about his previous homeland and life, about which only you can tell him right now to help him grow fast, physically, mentally and emotionally.

"He will be very advanced. He has to be because of the valuable mission that awaits him, as is our support to help him grow in his soul. He will project his mental images into material fulfillment in the form of success. Although material success as expression of soul growth is not the right way in our sense, we have to accept and support it in the souls with whom we have a bond so that they can radiate their mission of love and peace in a way less advanced souls can understand and become followers of the idea. That is our goal.

"Don't be ashamed to ask for help. If it supports the right path and helps others, you will always get it, as you know.

"Our bond means to help in love, in peace, to free souls of material thinking and to ready them for their blueprint paths of soul growth and acknowledgment of eternity. It means to direct them to accept and follow the path of the universal laws, of the universal mind and consciousness into eternity. Don't forget that and radiate it into your materialistic world. Communicate this idea telepathically to Jon when he visits to prepare him for his mission to radiate love, peace and strength into his surrounding and to whomever he meets as future leader in the world to which he has chosen to return.

"Love you Erika, Frumm."

* * *

Ruppert rewinds and labels the tape. As he places it on the shelf next to others, he turns to Erika. "Do you feel a little more reassured now that even Frumm says it's ok to let her listen to the tapes?" He crosses the room and sits in a chair across from her, picks up his coffee mug.

"Yes and no. On some levels, yes, but I also feel so very pressured." She takes a sip, puts down her mug.

"You still don't trust her? Not completely? Or do you not trust yourself?"

She slows at his words, considers them again. "Well, yes, I do, and yet I'm uneasy. Once I've given them up, I've let go of any control over them, and then what?"

"I think it'll be alright. I think she'll do the right thing."

"Well, we'll see." And then, all at once, a determined glint slips into her eye and she reaches for the phone, hesitates just a moment, looking at the clock, then dials.

"Hello Iris? How's it going?"

"Same old baby stuff, but better all around, thanks."

"Listen, when I come up next weekend, I'll bring some of the tapes with me. In fact, Ruppert has a case with lock and handle, I'll put them in that and you can go through them one by one, listen or transcribe or whatever you see fit to do, up to you."

"Really?" Iris' surprised cadence is followed by silence that seems to stretch forever. "That'd be terrific. Wow." A moment's stumble smothered within her own heart, and she listens into her daughter's joy. "I can't wait! Thank you so much for trusting me with them."

"I'll see you Thursday morning."

"I love you, Ma. See you then."

"What made you change your mind?" Ruppert asks as she hangs up the phone. He waits into the quiet; she shrugs, picks up her coffee again, takes a sip without answering. "Well, I'm proud of you. Whatever your reasons. You won't share them with me?"

She picks up a piece of toast on the plate, bites into it, glints her eyes at him, a quick shake of the head through chews, sloppy grin.

"Ok, then," he says, eyes sparkling over the top of his glasses. "Want some juice?"

"In a minute." A strong vibration fills the space around her, different sense from Frumm, heavier somehow. She gets up, quickly snatches the recorder from the bedroom, returns to her spot on the couch, turns on the microphone, catches Ruppert looking on silently.

* * *

New Friend

January 24, 1992

"Erika, you don't know me. I'm a friend from previous times, a friend of yours and Joseph's. This is the first time you have found my vibration pattern and I know it's confusing to you.

"Frumm wants to incarnate. He wants to help you, Joseph and your family, but he is not ready for incarnation at this moment. Maybe he will be later on. However, we want to keep him here because we need him here. We think it's more important he stays here with us and provides help to you and the world in the way he has done until now.

"Iris will be somewhat confused during the next few days. At this point, we don't know whether he can build the body of his soul or if he's ready to. He wants to be the soul of your future grandchild, Mary, to be close to Joseph and you throughout all these turbulent times, which will continue for the next few years.

"Be strong and continue on your way in setting and keeping up with your goals to provide support into your surroundings. I will contact you again, so don't be afraid. It was my first contact with you, therefore you felt me like a jolt. I will be more careful next time. I'm a friend, you will find my name sooner or later.

"I'll be back soon."

* * *

Erika shuts the recorder under Ruppert's watchful eye. "Is that how it happens?"

"Pretty much," she shrugs into herself, chuckles. "Felt him like a jolt? Rock is more like it, a rock pounding into my chest.

You know, that's what I'll call him next time he comes back. I'm guessing he won't mind."

"Rock?"

"Yes." When she turns to face him directly, her face is serious. "What do you think this means?"

"Sounds like there's another child coming. A Mary. And seems that Frumm wants to be it."

A smile creeps into the corners of her mouth. "This is unbelievable, utterly unbelievable." The words whistle out, and leave her just there.

"Want to call her back?"

"No!" she says, her eyes wide in mock-horror. "No way. She may not be ready, she may not know yet. I have to let her tell me, not the other way around. Anyway, sounds like he hasn't yet made the decision anyway, so she wouldn't yet be pregnant, right?"

"Could be. This is getting interesting."

CHAPTER 37

Help On The Way

February 8, 1992

Erika, I have decided to reincarnate. We have decided that I'm strong and determined enough for this, my last incarnation in your world as your granddaughter Mary. Whatever you name her will be fine with me, but keep it in the sense of Mary, in the sense of a young woman who carries the future of that world in her heart.

"She will give birth to a new idea in this future world. She will have a sense of idealism, convinced of the ideas of love, peace, strength, beauty and passion. These are her expressions of learning experiences of an earthly life, retold from a previous time into this future time of unity, with the possibility to unify the religions and races in the human world.

"This is her path into the universe of her existence, unifying universes unknown to you with vibration levels unfamiliar to you but known to me, which will be acknowledged in my future.

"My knowledge and experiences of this dimension will benefit all of you, as will my knowledge of the past. Once Mary is grown, this knowledge will come through for all of you as signs and acknowledgement of the peace, love and strength of the unified souls in a unified universe. It will radiate as the vibration of love and peace and the vibration of strength in the knowledge of the only truth for which you are searching.

"By then, the knowledge will exist on Earth, once we get past the momentary confusion, anger and pain, which are the result of not accepting and acknowledging that the only path of souls is their search for the truth. In love and peace, truth will lead the soul back to its Creator, the universal consciousness, which is the compound of all consciousnesses combined, as foundation of our acceptance of the universal laws to fulfill the vibration of truth and oneness, in the melding of all vibrations into the path of the only truth vibration which is composed of love, peace, forgiveness and strength.

"To be part of that is my goal, as it is yours and Joseph's, and Iris's and Bill's, who give us our physical body in acceptance of love and peace on the path to the eternity of truth, the eternal goal of knowledge for all of us. Once we reach maturity to accept this goal at our free will, which includes the search for the truth, the laws, the universal consciousness, the oneness in ourselves, then we will acknowledge the eternal vibration of truth no matter what happens.

"I am very, very happy, Erika. I will build a beautiful body for my soul to express my search for the truth in your world on my path into eternity. Give my love to Iris and Bill and Joseph. He knows already.

"Some of my friends will contact you. Don't be afraid. I could convince them that it is my free will to return in love and peace. They will support us and promised to carry on our bond. Believe in me and our friends.

"Love you, Frumm."

*　　*　　*

"What do you think?" Erika and Ruppert are both staring at the recorder as the tape clicks to its stop early Sunday morning. "What do you think?" Erika asks again.

"I think you should call Iris and find out. That's what I think."

Erika checks the clock. "Too early. It's not even eight."

Ruppert's face twists sardonically. "That wouldn't bother them. They have a little boy, remember? If I know anything, I know he's up!"

Erika chuckles. "I guess I could wait until eight-thirty," she says just as the phone rings.

"Iris! We were just talking about you. How are you?"

"Fine Ma. Jon and Bill are fine, too."

"Good. Look, I have those tapes ready for you. There are some other ones that just came through recently, I'll bring those as well."

"Ok. Good. I'm looking forward to them. By the way, I may be pregnant again. I'm not sure yet, but I think I might be. It would be a great start for this new year and Jon'll be almost three when the little one comes, so they could be great friends, I hope. We've been talking about it for a while, so this may be it."

She hears the words and happiness surges within her. "Hey, that's wonderful news! How exciting! When will you know for sure?"

"Within the week, I guess." Iris's voice sounds guarded to her mother, although Erika's joy seems to infect the edges of her sounds. "I'm excited, too."

"Oh, please call me right away, I can't wait. One of the tapes I got is about you again, but I'll let you listen to it yourself."

"Ok, sounds good. Look I hear Jon crying, so let me call you a little later."

"Bye, honey." Erika hangs up the phone, joy relishing from her face and eyes into the entirety of her being, charging it with a brilliance she hadn't imagined possible. The feeling remains in her heart the rest of the day, infecting everyone she touches, spreading the warmth with a sense of hope that reaches further than she could ever imagine.

CHAPTER 38

Reflections

February 15, 1992

Erika, here is Joseph, the reflection of Joseph as you have known him, as he will be in your memory forever, and as you want your grandson to know him, as his past. For that reason I want you to remember Joseph as the vibration of love, the philosopher, the poet. My reflection exists in remembrance of the time and space in which we both lived, and in which we live now as reflections from our world and dimension into your world and dimension.

"I still love you as I always have, with the love that is the vibration in which two souls vibrate in wholeness and unity. That unity can never be severed once it has become whole as a part of the fulfillment of the vibration of universal love within universal laws. We experienced this twice in your memory. Once in Atlantis during our life together, the other time in a remembrance of that past life in your feelings for me and our feelings as parts of a unit striving for wholeness again.

"You have built a barrier which only I, Joseph, can overcome in my wish for fulfillment with you, my other half, to reach the next dimension together with you. Therefore, I have built a reflection of our love and unity in that dimension. It is this reflection you are touching now, a reassurance of the universal truth in our soul and our wholeness, even though we are still, but not completely, divided again.

"Now, I am with you as your grandson, reincarnated as Jon, and, little by little, the memory in both of you will unite you again, triggered by the reflection from other dimensions as it is written and impressed in the Akashic records for eternity. You can call on them to remember, using your urge to fulfill your path in peace and strength as the key to open the door.

"We exist as multi-dimensional consciousnesses in multi-dimensional space according to multi-dimensional laws. When we fulfill one step in the right direction and pass into the next dimension, our vibration travels on as thoughtforms and ideas, in your language. They fill the universe of those dimensions and reflect further into other dimensions. They also reflect into your present universe, where they live as dreams. But for you, today, they are reality, the reality of my dimension melded with the reality of your dimension now and therefore we are united in wholeness again. Your grandson Jon, my future in your dimension, is included with your past of Olivia, my love from a former time. The connection of Joseph to Erika as vibration of love to Olivia exists in the same time and space as your current dimension.

"You cannot completely understand it at the moment, but trust me, it works this way. Therefore, part of me, my reflection, has come back to you now to reassure you of the reality of your world and the reality of my world as part of your world.

"I also want to reassure you that the reality of that world in which I live is part of me. You, Ophelia-Olivia, live here too, as a reflection and a part of Erika. You are not completely whole because the part of Erika is missing. The experiences of Erika will complete the unit of Olivia to allow her to become whole once more in that dimension through her unity with me.

"It needs time. As I need time to achieve the experiences and success of bringing the idea of love and peace to planet Earth through my reincarnation as Jon. I will fulfill my pathway of your grandson's bright future. Then I will be fulfilled and whole again in oneness through love. And in love to you, Olivia, in your final earthly path of learning experiences, acknowledgment and knowledge combined with Erika in the last stage of her second incarnation in one lifetime.

"You have finally started to recognize the importance of my messages, my sessions to you, Erika. With it, you awoke the vibration of my reflection in another dimension to reflect my love and trust to you. Now pass it on to your grandson. Give him all the experiences of our lives together in the vibration of love and peace. It will help him grow up in that vibration and fulfill his incarnation time on planet Earth in the never-ending cycle of the vibration of love and peace.

"You will again help me vibrate into my wholeness as the vibration of love and peace and, glowing like a bright star, into that other dimension I have known. It is the dimension of which Frumm had a glimpse and which Rock is longing for. It is where they work on themselves to reach the goal of their higher self by giving up their goal as Frumm did to voluntarily reincarnate on Earth to support you and me. He returned to keep his eternal bond with us. As reward for his courage, his inner self reflects as a bright star in that dimension, shining and growing on the pathway to eternity.

"I have the feeling you will understand, Erika, because you are trying so hard to fulfill your part of the bond. As I told you all the time, we will help you and we will support you to reach your goal in soul growth. Reassured, my love?

"Frumm will soon be Mary. Right now, he is working on his reflection into the next dimension, after which he will build the earthly body of his idea of Mary.

"I love you very much, Olivia-Erika. You have again started to return to your pathway to eternity. Joseph."

* * *

An abyss of sadness has cracked open within Erika's heart, still brimming with hope and love and patient waiting. Tears glide freely from her eyes, blurring her vision, taking the searing ache with them, settling it within herself. This loss, this terribly untouchable sense of loss engulfs her again, the one from another time when he had to leave her behind and she again hardened herself so she could bear it. And now, so near and yet unreachable and separated, she feels it again, and knows this is the sadness that has built the barrier over the last several weeks, tightened the shell around her heart so it wouldn't burst altogether.

She sits in embracing silence as tears well unending, and can barely breathe. *Is this it, is this really so?* Ache settling alongside Joseph's message deep within her, as she holds the reflection of his love in her mind and herself and knows she needs to let it go. Oh how it hurts, this need of leaving and distance, this void it carves within her, the loss of this love. She takes a deep breath and then another, hoping to clear her pain and her mind.

"Is this really the end?" She asks Ruppert after they listen to the tape once more. She catches herself holding herself bound tightly, realizing she'd hoped it would hurt less this second time. The tickle of a lone tear fleets down her cheek and she wipes it away casually as she turns to him. "I didn't do enough with it, I took it for granted, I lost it all again." She can't help the frost settling around her shoulders, this cold touch chilling her insides.

"No, hon, don't think like that. You did what you could in the time you had with him, with them. And maybe this isn't the end of it all. They promised to be around, to help and assist you, to give you the strength you need. And if all you feel is their presence, allow yourself to soak it in, don't turn it away. You are loved, please know that. Please be assured of that. Not just by me, but by them, and it seems there are many of them who love you and want to tend to you." His eyes caress her tiredness, and she glides into the comfort, allowing herself to soften just a little

"Nothing comes through anymore. I know it's my sadness over my loss, I seem to be blocking it out. I don't know why I do that." She shudders, prying loose a fragment of time, pulling it from the depths. "I think because I'm afraid to lose more, so I block it out so this loss can't happen from their end, so I'm the one to end it. How silly of me? I have cherished the messages, but I took them for granted, thinking I'd have him forever, after all, as spirit or soul or entity, isn't he timeless? I never fathomed I could lose him to reincarnation on Earth, to his incarnation as baby, my grandson, this little being who's so very far away, not only in miles but also in mind and his inability to speak at his age." She turns on a whisper, this tender hurt in her eyes still. "He's in there, I know, but I can't reach him or talk with him or see or speak with him, because he's a baby and who knows how much of his essence he will retain as he grows? Will he be totally different from the soul I've been speaking with, who's been gifting me with such treasures? And I never realized how valuable, how important these would be to me. I never imagined they would end. Oh Ruppert, how I've messed this up."

"But honey, you didn't. You couldn't do more than you did, don't you see that? You get to learn too, it takes time, you're on the path, he's told you that. Please don't despair. I can't see you beat yourself up like this, please, Erika. You're doing ok, you've always done ok with all this. Please believe me."

Her eyes have emptied into the void, and she can barely speak through them. "But I miss him so much," she exclaims, holding tightly onto Ruppert, unable to stir. "And yes, he'll grow up and might very well be an extraordinary person, but will I be able to witness any of it? Will I be alive? Or will I be called back before? I'm no fool when it comes to my illness, this disease that I'm never sure we've defeated completely. What if?"

"Love, don't. Let's take it one day at a time. We've been through so much already, you know you've got me by your side, and we'll get through this also. We'll do it together, you and me, and will make time to see Joseph, Jon grow up. We'll spend time and you'll get to know him and he'll get to know you. And you can shower him with all that love you have inside and he'll know who you are."

A tranquil moment slides into Erika as her eyes look far into the distance. "Yes, yes, you are right. We have been blessed." She looks out beyond, seemingly counting all the blinking lights. "Just yesterday I called Iris and told her that Frumm was hoping to have a name in the sense of Mary," she says through teary eyes. "You know what she told me?" He holds her gaze, waiting. "She told me she was planning to call the baby Mary if it's a girl." The wisp of a smile slides into her tears, lighting it momentarily with the glow of a thousand candles reaching the blue of her eyes. "It's going to be fine," she says, then slows. "No, it's going to be exquisite."

CHAPTER 39

Yet More Beginnings

Erika passed on July 31, 1998 after a brief, but final bout with her illness.

While traveling in Germany with her son during the months of May and June, she accidentally tripped on an uneven floor, and fell flat down. The brittleness of her bones, caused by recurrent chemotherapy treatments, could not withstand the fall: on impact, she broke her nose, one arm, her hands and her feet. She also hairline-fractured her shoulder, causing excruciating pain. She somehow endured the plane ride back to Florida with numerous casts, her son by her side.

Ruppert had been staying with us in New York and was anxious to return home after the news of her ordeal. The children were still in school throughout June; we were afraid to let him fly back on his own because a stroke two years earlier had robbed his short-term memory. Instead, we drove him (and the kids and the dog) home during the first weekend in July. Florida's wildfires closed parts of I-95, forcing a five-hour detour onto the long drive, but we finally got him home.

Although Erika's bones healed slowly and steadily, recovery was spotty. Mental anguish over her husband's frail health (created by flawed monitoring following a conversion of an irregular heartbeat, resulting in the stroke two days later that wiped out his short-term memory) and disputes over the sale of her clinic around that time, wore her down. Although she loved life and her will was strong, the adverse situations gnawed at her insides.

I always believed that, given the chance, she would will anything into being. True to her spirit, she fought on with incredible courage and strength, the lioness fighting for her cubs, determined to spend more time with her loved ones in her quest to fulfill her mission and goal to be loving, giving, ever-wise Olivia.

We love you, Mom. Thank you for all: for your ever-present courage and strength to carry on, your ever-enduring love for us all. You've touched each one of us, you've touched our hearts, you've left your spark in us and with us. We will carry your love with us forever and will carry on for you, spreading love, peace and harmony into this world.

October 2, 1998.

ACKNOWLEDGEMENTS

This book could not have come to be without the support and love of many people: My family, my friends, first and foremost. Thank you for your faith in me.

The members of Hayes Jacobs' Writing Seminar were my support group for many of the early years. You guided my steps with your thoughtful comments and critiques, allowing me to hone my craft in a safe setting. Thank you.

Mina Roustayi, my earliest of readers, ploughed through the roughest of the versions. Thank you for your kind endurance! Karli Kelber and Thomas Bobowicz read my latest. Thank you for your words of wisdom and encouragement and invaluable introspection.

Sunshine, my very good friend and real-time shaman, foretold the birth of this book many years ago. I've held onto your words all the time and never stopped believing!

My family has carried me throughout the years with love and belief in me, even when they didn't understand what I was doing. Thank you for your unquestioning support and encouragement and incredible patience. I love you more than I could ever express in words or otherwise.

A child is raised by a village, a book in much the same way. Even from beyond I've felt your help, Mom and Dad, your guidance, and your unwavering support. I hope you are smiling!

ABOUT THE AUTHOR

Born in Germany, Iris Struller arrived in Miami, Florida with her parents at age thirteen. She brought with her a love for writing, birthed with a fifth grade class assignment that asked her to weave a story around three unrelated words. She found she could actually see the magic unfold, as her imagination painted a detailed picture.

Window to the Soul is her first book. She is currently working on her second, a partial memoir that explores the repercussions of childhood trauma on life decisions and a path to healing.

When she's not writing, she's painting in her studio. You can find some of her work on www.irisbeate.com

Made in the USA
Middletown, DE
09 June 2019